INTRODUCTION

This book is based on "The Day of the Lobbyist" a Plutocratic fraternity of palm greasing accuracy afforded fraud to ascend beyond the trillion-dollar mark. David Walker the Director of GOA introduced the Federal Budget in 2008 as an unsustainable burning platform. The Bill of Rights in its collective nobility that constitutes the Amendments of "we the people", not the Individual Conglomerate.

The First Amendment, the right of the people peaceably to assemble, and to petition the Government for a redress of grievances, except the Supreme Court rendered "we the people eclipsed by the Individual Corporation as a living breathing person. Therefore, the Lobbyist under the first amendment afforded Wall Street Conglomerates a predominate influence over the American Voter."

Disillusion without a Vote:

The American vote became null and void, like that old west novel, "Disillusion." The town folk held silent, arrogance disengaged an authoritative edge of the first amendment, presumptuous was overbearing in manor, the crier forth with rang intent, a contemptuous siege demanding obedience, levitated the ultimate seconds, into a flight of the Super Pac, billion intimidates. Bentley Robes partisans garbed cross the barrier, endowed Wall Streets a custom-made first amendment, with an Individual Corporation given rights, to redress grievances, in 1999 Congress abolish the Glass-Steagall Act that regulated Wall Street and

America disengaged! There's the question what is considered excessive, cause and effect, lets count the ways; Congress left town for five weeks and didn't give a damn! While 8.3 unemployed remained, providing a human necessity is not socialism it's compassion. Livestock producers, tree farmers left to rupture in the breach of confidence. $110 billion in automatic cuts, military, education and the death rattle of domestic programs gaze beyond terminal, a bipartisan solution of five weeks to contemplate what really matters. Wall Street top 1% yearly financial wealth in 2012 had increased from 15% to an excess of 25% in less than thirty years. And yet Wall Street in nature possesses a self-portrayed theatrical allusion of the Constitutional bearing "we the people, cloaked behind the grasp of monetary quarterly addiction. Wall Street the opium phantom of benevolence dispensing billion for Congressional influence, altruism impales an exhibit of entitlement, we don't tax the wealthy 1%! A bi-partisan Congressional fiscal reform commission, flexed it's intent without the financial resources, affording Wall Street a masterful self-indulgence of a billion-dollar club reflecting zero tax as the ultimate Demi-God of attainment.

Fairy dust and a Trillion dollar rip off!

Moody's and S&P seal of triple AAA ratings clutched the wings of the Subprime Global mortgage scavenger that trumpeted the voracity of foreclosures, thanks to Congress for ignoring S&P and Moody's deceptive sham. It was Congress who considered fraud without intent was not a criminal act, affording Wall Street traders to insure toxic subprime mortgages without thought of consequence or honor! Commission first!

"A pivotal commitment, America first!"

Patrick Henry orated, "We are obligated to revaluate our Ideals; Our Country was fashioned by the valor of our forefathers, they accepted the autumn of revelation, freedom and equality to rise above subjugation. Mr. President, it is natural for man to indulge in the illusions of hope. We are apt to shut our eyes against a painful truth, and listen to the song of that siren till she transforms us into beasts. Is this the part of wise men, engaged in a great and arduous struggle for liberty?" Patrick Henry vowed with pivotal commitment, "Give me liberty or give me death."

An elite group that September day in 1787, signed the Constitution, the youngest Jonathan Dayton 26, and Benjamin Franklin was a youthful 81. We the People of the United States In order to form a more perfect Union! Establish Justice, insure domestic Tranquility, provide for the common defense, promote the general Welfare, and secure the Blessings of Liberty to ourselves and our, Posterity. The Great depression of 1929 illustrated a hemisphere of abandonment that transformed us into beasts of prey that gave birth to Glass-Steagall act. In 1999 Wall Street Banking, Insurance and the Securities Industry spend billion and abolished the Glass-Steagall Act of 1933, and the fix was in!" The Lobbyist consolidated a billion dollar-financial strategy into a fraudulent scheme of trillions, it required sixty-three years, four months and twenty-eight days to set forth the Twenty first Century Déjà vu, known as the Financial Services

Modernization Act of deregulation! "Mark Twain" said it best, " No man's life, liberty, or property are safe while the congress is in session."

Human rights; the autumn of revelation:

Every man, woman and child in America should have the inalienable equality of all human rights. Education is a "birth-right" of monumental perception; knowledge is the bridge of evolution that formulates the mind and character to enhance the responsibility of an individual from one generation to another. Its technical sense of responsibility is to bestow and advance skills and values for the growth of a greater nation. How in God's name, do we selectively by the weight of an individuals financial status, eliminate educational programs and Teachers salaries, the Pell grants for college students, the Peace Corps and the National Endowment for the Arts have become terminal in value.

Introduction   Page One trough Four

CHAPTER ONE

Unemployment 8.3, as poverty increases:

Eighty percent of Americans financial wealth is controlled by seven percent of the affluent and fifteen percent of the affluent controls the net worth; and guess who owns Seventy Three percent of total personal debt, the bottom seven percent! Twenty-five Hedge Fund executives in 2009 earned in excess of a billion dollars personal incomes, thanks to the policy making Legislative lack of responsibility. The wealthiest1% invests billion playing the persuasion game, "let's bankrupt America for personal gains." That's not the great American dream, that's criminal! Several thousand Corporate Executives simply committed fraud; Congress said it was without intent! Therefore it's not a criminal act! Congress preventing the course of justice is a punishable crime, have you heard the term without intent as absolution! "We the Corporation" thanks to the Supreme Court devoured the existence of "We the people"! And guess what, it was with intent! And 2.1 million youths went homeless, and yet Congress has no insightful hypothesis how to rectify, try establishing an apprentice draft work force to revitalize our infrastructure, draft American youth's into an educational work force, 50% in 2012 have limited skills for survival, the Army won't accept them, but gangs are dedicated to devour that 50% of our American Youth.

Ex Service started with 21 million:

Congress finds billion to support an independent Ex Service Military Organization, which has become an independent Army, or a Gang of professionals for hire. In 2003 Blackwater's first contract was 21 million plus, 2005 they had a two year contract increased to 106 million that extended in 2006 to 488 million plus, protective services personnel increased beyond the mark of insanity, specialists, translators, intelligence analysts, Blackwater's personal leased equipment increased. Blackwater's 5 fully armored vehicle lease invoice, 491,328 thousand not including 68,672 for maintenance, on the mentioned five vehicles. Now from May 2007 to May 2009, Blackwater had increased their contract cost to 791 million plus. That had nothing to do with contracts listed as Task Orders, 7, 8 and 9 they were awarded to Triple Canopy, Blackwater, and DynCorp received 113,160,844 million plus, Task Order 10 was awarded to Blackwater that ended on September 3. 2008 was 107,120,799 million. Blackwater Task Orders 1, 6, 8 and 10 total was a billion and counting.

2012 the Pentagon and Xe Services:

The Pentagon is the world's largest five story office building, six million five hundred square feet, approximately 23,000 military and civilian employees and as for non-defense support personnel, they participate from within the Pentagon ranging from three or four thousand into the unknown, guess what! In the Twenty First Century McDonalds has also invaded the Pentagon, including twenty or thirty other fast food outlets like, Dunkin Donuts, Starbucks, KFC, Pizza Hut, Subway, Blackwater and Halliburton and the list goes on and on, you can't believe the traffic at lunch time, the only term that fits the massive humanity in motion, "Halliburton and fast food!"

President Obama proposed to increase the Pentagon budget by 4 percent, [wink, wink] to $534 billion. The war in Afghanistan and Iraq in 2011 expenditure exceeded a trillion, that's if you include outsourcing. HR 1540 Section 1021-1022 National Defense Authorization Act, authorized additional $662 billion for anti- terrorism within the United States and abroad, secrecy intensifies, arrogance behind close doors without specific allocated spending. There are more dots depicting the United States involvement around the globe. To be specific, the most accurate count is somewhere between 1,075 or even 1,300 actually the number might even be higher, nobody knows for sure. Halliburton overcharged sixty one million dollars, that's chump change in the scheme of things; they also supplied gas and cokes. It would have been cheaper for President Obama to have picked up the phone and called Kuwait and said, "old buddy I need a favor." 2009, President Obama committed an additional 30,000 extra U.S. troops into Afghanistan, he flipped his hand back and forth from pronation to supination, and expressed his summation, it felt, he said, "it was just about the right mix; that's if Blackwater would supply a supplementary 50,000 to 55,000 auxiliary contractors." The cost factor take 55,000 personal time 1,222 dollars per day, that equates to 445,000 per individual per year and observe the billion-dollar hand increase into trillions in real time. Henry Waxman House Oversight Committee chair, submitted that the IRS had determined that Blackwater violated federal tax laws, when they listed an armed guard as an independent contractor. The implication Blackwater avoided paying millions in Social Security, Medicare, unemployment, by various illegal schemes. In 2009, The U.S. State Department informed Blackwater and the world, it will not renew the Iraq contracts, except, in 2010 they where awarded a $100 million contract from the CIA. And the Task Orders are heading towards 10. Hay! It was with intent!

Lobbyist Dividing the Spoils:

Diligence LLC Services, popped into existence in Baghdad in July 2003, Britain's Nick Day former MI5 Intelligence agent and one of the head honchos. They have experts in international law, journalism and an access of 100 former intelligence service employees. They are related to New Bridges Strategies, for they share many of the same board members. CEO Mike Baker a former covert operator for the CIA. Food for thought, why did Diligence form a LLC, it combines the tax flexibility of a partnership and personal liability protection, and requires no US citizenship or permanent residence, there is no required regulation to hold annual meetings or record meetings and can be owned by individuals or other Companies.

Richard Burt, chairman of Diligence Quoted, "The opportunity for business growth in the Middle East has never been better."

Ed Rogers vice Chair of New Bridge Strategies and Diligence is co-founder of BG&R, Barbour, Griffith and Rogers Lobbying firm, its operating philosophy, "performance based: a proactive, creative approach to solving problems and aggressively seeking results." This might be hard to conceive, they share the same DC office right down the street from; you guessed it, the White House. Rogers served under the Reagan Administration, and Bush 41 campaign. Joe Allbaugh Deputy Chairman of Diligence, served as National Campaign Manager for the Bush-Cheney 2000 election. It's amazing how in seventy years the Lobbyist influence has complicated the Pentagon's position on war by dividing up the spoils. The death of one additional military American youth is a Political absurdity and should be classified as a criminal act. Iraq had no nuclear weapons, Afghanistan the land of unachievable conquest, Alexander The Great, Genghis Khan the British and Russia failed; yet antiquity should have informed President Barack Obama to get the hell out yesterday. The bloodied envelope addressed to President Obama, you have boots on the ground in 117 nations; 110 of those nations have less than a percentage point of the world population while our young Hero's are still dying in Iraq and Afghanistan for the love of country. We are paying the independent Services security personal 600 dollars a day; they are trained by American Tax payers and will fight for the highest bidder. The fact of Blackwater loyalty has bypassed paying millions in Social Security, Medicare, unemployment and related taxes, it's beneath their legal responsibility. Xe Services, Blackwater Mercenary have no accountability they are beyond the reach of the Constitution, yet their units have the ability to unleash indiscriminate violence. The Scariest reality was during New Orleans Hurricane Katrina they appeared like Ninja fighters or the SS in Black uniforms patrolling the streets, heavily armed, they appeared with an air of Authority, they have taken a single oath it's to the highest bidder, not the Constitution. No matter how you package Blackwater, Xe Services they are a Mercenary army being paid by American Tax payers. Their Lobbying force is commendable in palm-greasing effect.

Xe Services largest private Security Contractor:

Mr. President your administration awarded Blackwater's Xe Services a quarter of a billion dollars to aid the US State Department and the CIA in Afghanistan and twenty two hot spots, the world's most aggressive Mercenary Army started with the approval of the United State Senate, with an expenditure of a 6.5 Million budget, now Blackwater's leading Lobbyist are escalating into the billion and growing. Blackwater's leading lobbyist, the K Street Republican firm Alexander Strategy Group, founded by former senior staffers of Tom DeLay, have applied for operating licenses in all of the coastal states of the United States. Mercenary value increased into the billion, Education not so much; they took a reduction in budget!

A vote of confidence:

In 2011 former NSA head & CIA exec Inman became one of two head directors. Ted Wright became CEO; the company named Suzanne Folsom its chief regulatory and compliance officer. High profile lobbyist former White House Counsel Jack Quinn states, "I am proud to join and help lead Xe Services, "The men and women demonstrate their dedication, professionalism I am honored to support them."

A slight problem:

Baghdad shooting killed 17 people, and two Blackwater contractors imprisoned for the May 2009 deadly shooting in Kabul,

Afghanistan. April 16, 2010, Blackwater/Xe violated federal law on felony weapons charges, providing unlawfully weapons and military equipment overseas. Blackwater/Xe Lobbyist escalated their power base throughout the world, including the United States. The indictment alleged that officials falsified documents hundred of times, how accurate are the indictments, in August 2010, Blackwater/Xe agreed to pay a $42 million fine to settle. However, President Obama did awarded a quarter of a billion dollars after the facts. Blackwater/Xe was picked by the Department of Defense; Counter-Narcotics Technology Program Office acquired a five-year contract for equipment, material and services, in support of counter-narcotics activities. The contract exceeds $15 billion. John Ashcroft, President George W. Bush's attorney general hired as Ethic Chief, a superior ploy for Lobbyist to secure billion. They manufactured the grizzly APC a 22 Blackwater High Threat Armor Protection System, their Airships a remote piloted designed aircraft, their tentacles are flexible in training mercenaries, to supplying weapons, to the highest bidder. The Government spent billion on trained American Ex military personal that Blackwater indoctrinated into the World Secret Military Organization that has no loyalty to the Constitution, yet our Legislators have afforded them the Authorization to invade every aspect of our Government Security System, We just might wake up one morning and find Xe Services LLC instead of the Stars and Stripes. Don't kid yourself they operate in secrecy.

"61" Million an oversight:

Food for thought, Cheney expressed his opinion when

asked about Halliburton relocation inside Dubai said, "Its part of a strategy to concentrate Halliburton efforts in the Middle East, in order to attract business". I thought his business was the Middle East, and that included the American Tax payer pocketbook. Halliburton overcharged 61 million for gas being supplied in Iraq. The intent, was an honest mistake, they have a proficiency, for oversight, it's called, "You got to be kidding! That happened again." A Note of interest, Halliburton's Chairman and CEO David J Leser, salary was 2.26 million plus compensation. He's responsible for the welfare of 50,000 employees in seventy countries, now that's a tuff turf to haul!

The thought of stupidity!

The Real Estate Portal, an elaborate resource of global financial stability squandered by fraudulent deception, during that time interest rates consumed the financial soul of America, indebtedness escalated into personal bankruptcy, the credit lure of Utopia, an affordability with the sweet allure of almost zero interest, as winter exceled without a single thought of upsurge into oblivion, Congress extends the fraudulent appendage of deficit; millions of Americans unknowingly escalated into foreclosure, indebtedness of a lifetime, Medical insurance and hospitalization became unattainable! The thought of down right stupidity! Deregulate Wall Street once again, that's equivalent to a cerebral affliction of malignant, Congress should pay attention regarding Einstein's quote of Insanity, doing the same thing over and over again and expecting different results, that's the Legislative house of instant gratification, repeats insanity; 26 million became unemployed, 4 million have endured unemployment beyond a year, that's exempt from the 2.1 million homeless youth. Worker pension funds squandered without a prayer, the wake of fraudulent intent extended foreclosure beyond global financial stability, yet Wall Street traders made billion, as millions endured food stamps, Veterans on second and third tours bestowed with disability, foreclosure and unemployment, Congress policymakers the folly of ignorance, the endowment of special favors for the wealthy 1%. GE proudly expressed their billion-dollar team of tax experts; zero taxes and moved their financial heart and bottom line to China. An idiom of deducible reasoning, made in America shipped to China; we call it greed envy or GE.

The "**Hype**" before Tuesday, the Lobbyist ruled:

President Herbert Hoover inauguration speech in March 1929, "Given the chance to go forward with the policies of the last eight years, we shall soon with the help of God, be in sight of the day when poverty will be banished from this nation." And yet the handwriting was looming behind close doors. Hindsight has value, only if you pay attention! From 1929 to 1941 one third of our work force was unemployed. A chicken in every pot, except the chicken left the Country. What overrides the intellectual process of repeating insanity time and time again! Congress!

Thomas Jefferson's perception:

If the American people ever allow private banks to control the issue of their money, first by inflation and then by deflation, the banks and corporations that will grow up around them, will deprive the people of their property until their children will wake up homeless on the continent their fathers fought and died for."

Déjà vu, a quote!

A little group of willful men, representing no opinion but their own, rendered the great government of the United States helpless and contemptible. In 2012 those words still ring true. The quote was from Woodrow Wilson the year1912:

Jobs the Nourishment and essence of necessity:

Jobs the essential ingredient for physical and cerebral proliferation, a daily requirement to thrive vigorously with life's intoxication and unlimited possibilities. The greatest stigma to mankind, a child goes hungry, while the few endeavor on self-indulgence. That's the influential having a sense of self-identity; all others have no soul or the right of existence. Democratic or Republican is not the right to forgo a conscience of Social responsibility for all Americans. Our Forefathers brought forth the concept of justice, that all men are created equal! Social morality, the bottom line all men are not created equal, they call themselves the wealthy 1%.

3 million Americans are the 1% fraternity of wealth:

Jack Abramoff was quoted, "I was actually thinking of

writing a book, the idiot's guide to buying a congressman, you do realize, that most congressmen don't feel they're being bought. Most congressmen, I think, can in their own mind justify the system." The reformed Abramoff's total detached honesty is that of a defunked Lobbyist.

A prose, a Lobbyist, by Mot:

There was once a man of corruption; noted for his slick stick of persuasion with label Lobbyist renowned, notorious was he, without a hick-cup of hesitation, corruptly in tune for betrayal without tribe of intent perfectly legal, I submit without legislative effect, integrity not pictorial principals breached. Abramoff was a Lobbyist of repute with confinement he served his indiscretion, that's an unconscionable denominator for ethics incarcerated don't uphold Constitutional law! There was a Hedge Fund Executive who purchased insurance, and bet against himself, and received a Billion dollars and he buried the Billion in a loophole, his name John, and it was with intent!

Lobbyist A Wall Street Beast:

The predicament, "the day of the Lobbyist" it became the inflated practice of financial-deregulation. The benchmark of Wall Streets success the bottom line, we have 8.3 unemployed and the American workforce committed the cardinal sin, they demanded a living wage. Wall Street's apatite; extends the marrow of quarterly net profit. The Plutocratic Secret Society and their puppet Lobbyist theme song, "If you tax us, off shore we shall go!" Intellectual growth should commence at birth and cease only at death," "Einstein's insightful thought, that Legislators, once elected intellectual growth ceases and personal gratification prevails, profits looms foremost for the selected Demi-God's of Wall Street, God must have known Politian's and Lobbyist where not his finest creation.

Individual an adjective a mathematical quantity, One!

The US Supreme Court, yes they did! In their wisdom, elevated an Individual Corporation into a person of living renown, it revolutionized our first amendment, the US Supreme Court by definition dictated an Individual Corporation was transformed by converting an adjective into a noun, a distinction that is Ludicrous, life deals a variety of renditions; some exceptional, and some tragic, it's not always the power of the American majority that will determine the Constitutional interpretation. The US Supreme Court converted an adjective into "We the Corporation" the wizardry of an Individual Corporation trailblazing Wall Streets bottom line, profit!

"We the people," are now considered in text, neutered by the Supreme Court, that a Corporation, a single entity brilliantly misrepresented but somehow doesn't know the difference between an adjective and a noun or the uterus! It's not in the uterus where a Corporation develops between fifth and sixth month of its existence, it's in the bottom line of the quarterly profit numbers.

We the Individual Corporation!

The US Supreme Court amended the Constitution in
the literal sense, by altering the grammatical gender of absolute
from, "We the people." Congress afforded the Corporative
Lobbyist open-end Legislative privileges, modifying the realm of
the first amendment, the US Supreme Court in their wisdom
elevated a mythical adjective that revolutionized an Individual
Corporation to the status of "We the Corporation," it overrides "We
the people!" Chief Justice John Roberts stated his decision
intellectually Lawful! Historical fact, the Senate and House of
Representatives have always been seeded with partisan needs
first; therefore the term bipartisan is truly an art of cynical
disillusion. Wall Street In 2009 deregulated and upped the quota
to a hawkish 3.3 billion financial influence peddling, and 14,200
Lobbyist opened the flood gates of fraudulent resourcefulness that
brought America to its knees, Lehman Brothers went bankrupt,
Bear Stern spiraled into oblivion, and Merrill Lynch curled up to
Bank of America. The big- ten filed chapter 11 Bankruptcies,
besides Lehman Brothers, World Com, United Airlines, Pacific
Gas and Electric and Global Crossing they all had assets
exceeding 25 billion, try digesting that concept. August 2009
behind close doors the great debate bypassed the deficit, Capital
Hill introduced a dash of Flip Flop into a disorder that defines, "the
political system," a figure of speech in which statements can
become contradictory, depending on the terms of interpretation, a
festival of conviction, without a hiccup, that's dependent on the
value of underlying assets such as futures, simply put, the
Conglomerates wants tax welfare.

From what ever to the US Supreme Court:

Why vote when a Partisan US Supreme Court voted in their judicial astuteness affording the wealthiest to adjudicate their own finical agenda. Wall Street Trickle down economics a fable of distortion, the first amendment belongs to the wealthy 1%, they subsidize Congress, and influenced the Supreme Court, that an Individual Company is a living person, became a solitary unparalleled endeavor that opened the flood gates of deregulation, tax loophole and behind close doors elusion became the Lobbyist dominion, simply eliminated tax liabilities by relocating their financial gains off shore, with Congress approval.

1980 the playing field was balanced:

The election law of 1980 stipulated a playing field of equality, removing the Plutocratic financial influence. Jimmy Carter and Ronald Reagan both received $29.4 million each, Anderson the Independent received $18.5 million with allowance for private fund-raising to achieve a maximum of $29.4. What happened to the Ideology of doctrine, a fair playing field? Elections have become a market place to purchase Legislative and Congressional influence, thanks to the Bentley Robed partisan Supreme Court. In 2012 campaign contributions indorsing a third parties values slandering a candidate, it's called a Super PAC, the American Voter was given the god given right and responsibility to Vote; but in 2012 if you are talking about the real world; it's a complicity of unlimited contribution, what signifies intent of collusion from a Super PAC having financial domination, that obliterates America's Vote and principles? If you can spell Wall Street Lobbyist, you got your answer!" August 15, 2012 by all indications we will exceed the 1 billion mark in slanderous Campaign spending without a blue print of success.

The handwriting was on the wall in 1999:

Republican John Dingell the Dean of the House of Representatives America's Watchdog stated, that the banks in 1999 would become too big to fail, that it would result in a Government bailout, he laid out the blueprint for failure, and as usual nobody headed the actuality of 1929. John Dingell was quoted, repealing the Glass Steagall act would afford Wall Streets commercial banks, investment banks, Security firms and Insurance companies to deregulate and consolidate. They did! John was right! Words of wisdom from John, "This House is about as poisonous as I've ever seen it in my career, there is little room for moderates. It used to be that when we'd get a bill that we'd really need, we could always count on some across-the-aisle dealings. No more!" John Dingell evolved with the American youth, 18 to 35 agree with John and Ron Paul's honesty for America's survival. I'm pleased that Ron Paul spoke out, no double talk, or flip-flopping, or pleasing the cerebral dead.

Ron Paul should run as an Independent:

Ron Paul said, "I will simply remove five Cabinet departments, Energy, HUD, Commerce, Interior and Education.

Abolish the Transportation Security Administration and return responsibility for security to private property owners, abolish corporate subsidies, stop foreign aid, end foreign wars and return spending back to 2006 levels. I have a feeling Wall Street sat up, listened, and threw up!

Food for reflection:

The US Supreme Court Justice John Paul Stevens stated, "in a functioning democracy the public must have faith that its representatives owe their positions to the people, not to the Corporations." Chief justice of the Supreme Court John Roberts had a different summation; he interpreted the Super Pac, as an individual Plutocratic freedom of speech. I thought the vote was based on a even playing field, hell let's face it; an Individual's billions against a working mans limited financial expenditure is slightly a lopsided long shot, unless you are betting on a Wall Street Lobbyist. Then anything is possible, only if it's without intent!

"Individuals and Super Pac's! What is that?"

The Super PAC, Political Action Committee, and the US Supreme Court ruling, "Individual Conglomerates and Corporations are people!" Except we the people, are restricted in campaign contributions, now freedom of speech, affords the wealthy Plutocrat like Sheldon Adelson to contribute without monetary limitation, for campaign advertisement known as the Super Pac. Now a Harvard intellectual type asked, what if? "We transfer the Super Pac million dollar contribution to an independent third party, can that individual hurtle proviso attack ads into the absurd, answer, "you bet!" His friend inquired, "What else did they teach you at Harvard!" The answer, "freedom of speech, Ingratiate oneself with Constitutional Super PAC schmoozing, it's financially superior to perjury."

Super PAC in real time, "Winning Our judgement:"

A Vegas billionaire Sheldon Adelson a highly paid Executive of the Las Vegas Sands Co., an associate of Newt Gingrich, donated $5 million to a Super PAC designated, "Winning Our Future", introduced a video in South Carolina, "When Mitt Romney Came To Town," less than a sympathetic concept it was bankrolled by the Winning Our Future Super PAC, the message was "turning the misfortunes of others into   Mitt Romney's personal financial gains." The film interviewed people who lost their jobs. It's was controversial not productive and more than less accurate, as for the contribution try a different lever of political devotion, What the hell Sheldon stated, "lets fund Mitt, guess what! Sheldon Adelson, donated $ 10 million to Mitt Romney, he must have enjoyed watching Mitt Coming To Town!

Exhibits by Mitt and President Obama:

Mitt stated, "Corporations are people, my friend... of course they are. Everything corporations earn ultimately goes to the people. Where do you think it goes? Whose pockets? Whose pockets? People's pockets... Human beings, my friends." Then he went to Israel and the UK, enough said! President Obama Super dandy, "the private sector is doing fine." Mitt and President Obama both have an ability to create a Super blunder without spending a nickel. Sheldon Adelson could have saved $ 15million.

What's not Presidential!

Mitt said on the campaign trail, "I got gold in my heart! And for ten years I paid approximately 13% in Taxes, and Contributed 10% tax deductible towards Mormon charity. President Obama signed the table of confinement! "HR 1540 1021-1022 of concealment." President Obama declares he's against indefinite detention for American Citizens. You ever encountered the expression, if you sign it! You will use it! Ask Congress about McCarthy's witch hunt!"

A fact of truth:

James G. Blaine Congressman ran for President on the Party of Half Breeds, yeah the Political party did exist, when asked said, "The honor of the Lobbyist should not be taken lightly, nor should it eroded by a single fraudulent act." That sounded about right in 1864 for censure was like the old hound, that kept on sleeping till the diner bell or death did him partake. That Congressman James G. Blaine had informed President Lincoln the definition of the word single, when using the term Lobbyist, was a fraudulent statement, he smiled and said, Mr. President try a plethora, you know they are worse, then them their flies. That was the inspiration for my defunked attitude!

A Mathematical Myth:

Lets evaluate a mathematic theory of illiteracy into a curve of proper perspective, A trillion equals one thousand billion and a billion equals billionaire's, our Wealthiest 1% pay less than 15% Taxes ask Mitt, thanks to the Lobbyist Conglomerates we have a non- tariff for the Wealthiest 1%, simply put! They don't pay their fair share. Yet the Government will levy Teachers and the Education system to the short end of $38.6 billion in reduction. Student Loans mark the Trillion-dollar threshold of indebtedness, survey suggest 85% of Collage Grads are returning to the nest, home sweet home and apple pie. Ask Congress about their trough binging billion that's attached to the pork stick of persuasion. They are not the lawmakers who took a pledge to the Constitution and we the people! Balancing the budget a fairy tale, but pork on the other hand, compensates the wealthy few. I have listed two earmarks simply stuffed into a single bill that compensated both sides of the trough, $593,000 for research, why primates slinging their feces? Ask Congress they are the experts! 526,000 to study the effect cocaine has on the sex-drive of Japanese Quail; Congress decided to invest Pork in special education, 55,000 at Virginia University to study Jordanian Students, water pipe smoking habits, and one thing for sure, somebody was smoking something! A poor man doesn't give a damn about a Gorilla slinging feces, when our Supreme Court excelled at feces slinging ability towards the American majority. A billion on Super PAC's and not a single insightful conclusion that spending a billion will nullify the American vote, 93% of all additional Income earned in the USA is devoured by the wealthy top1% and not a supplemental cent for Education. That's a good start towards an additional trillion in Student loan debt at 6% or whatever! They will have a lifetime to repay the Government or Social Security will deduct if from their retirement fund. If you're fifty forget the thought of Social Security.

A Shakespeare vision!

"The day of the Lobbyist" includes a few deceased historical decades of observing the Lobbyist translate the Constitution for their Masters bidding. The main Character Thomas Mot, is a conglomerate of several individuals including yours truly, I'm Independent by life's journey, therefore call me Mot!

A prose, a Lobbyist, by Mot:

There was once a man of corruption; noted for his slick stick of persuasion with label Lobbyist renowned, notorious was he, without a hick-cup of hesitation, corruptly in tune for betrayal without tribe of intent perfectly legal, I submit without legislative effect, integrity not pictorial principals breached. Abramoff was a Lobbyist of repute with confinement he served his indiscretion, that's an unconscionable denominator for ethics incarcerated don't uphold Constitutional law! There was a Hedge Fund Executive who purchased insurance, and bet against himself, and received billion dollars and he buried the billion in a loophole, his name John, and it was with intent!

The birth of the Lobbyist:

The term Lobbyist was born into disrepute with mark of ink, a reporter in the latter eighteen hundreds, set to print, front page caption, "Sleaze a Lobbyist of intent!" They are a sordid type, corrupt in caucus manor, a sheath of secrecy lurks darkness, behind recesses of Legislative chicanery, palm-greasing peddler's are those of Political persuasion. A bit of trivia the term Lobbyist never forthright found existence in the first amendment text for it's a phantom that dictates its will by Wall Street finical influence, the Lobbyist an apparition of a ghostly amendment, spend billions with fraudulent intent!

The forbidden, 1867 the unsanctioned Lobbyist:

The Willard Hotel stood six stories in congressional splendor, for it was proclaimed, "The day of the Lobbyist," from within the majestic confines of nobility, emerged legislative patronizing palm-sprouting fellows of inducement, flag-bearing velvet drapes of equitable swathe bordered the Hotel Lobby, a buzz, the pertinence of hallowed amendments, trespassed congressional activities through its sanctified halls, where once resided revered Presidents, a fluted muse in partisan tune, was the Lobbyist lure, from the golden shovel a peddlers influence, concealed the agenda of lobbyist persuasion, a crows flight from gated stables, yet the sent rose to the occasion, the descending shadow sculptured the westerly morning radiance, across the White House South Portico a slothful path, ushered a carriage bearing upon the Willard Hotel, intense bell men tenaciously circle the lobby, for they are the wannabe sharks, a frenzy to snag a flavor of political chicanery, the litany of fundamental civil liberties, assented from the embassy, where greed and Lobbyist never slept, redress was entitlement, grievances tolled its banner wares, "Petition the Government for Redress of Deregulation". An unequivocal acuteness altered direction and interpretation for a select few, the Constitution beheld financial compensation for the influent of persuasion. A vision, a retractable scope to behold, 1867 a summer day bearing forthright a Lobbyist reputed with flare would arise in full pursuit from the Willard Hotel, stealth with thought of political corruption, it was the predators quest, an overture, a masterly alternative grin skillful reaped the mark of theatrical inspiration, three steeps a verbal lure, a diversion before passing, "Morning Senator!" A Shakespearean sway, with thrust of stature tipped his top hat, a versatile walking stick, candidly postured in front of his highly polished square-toe boots, obstructed the walkway, a left hand forthright unbuttoned the black frock coat a colorful silk sheen vest he laid bear, a flip of the wrist, in perfect pitch of dexterity, an infamous pocket watch was in full display, inquire would he, the precise second of time, the Lobbyist pinnacle web an ability to arbitrate drunk or sober, the art of political palm inducement while inquiring.

"Senator, I represent Central Pacific Railroad, and its essential that you are given the opportunity to enhance your position," accordingly the required necessity was financial inducement or a down right bribe. The stature of corruption was the Lobbyist arena of influence. Lobbyist would congregate in cigar smoked back rooms after the Civil War in 1866, a legendary yarn of a Railroad lobbyist, his professional handle was Jack Black Central; twisted as a one-legged deviate Sheriff, awaiting high noon for a twenty five dollar hanging. In his defense, the Lobbyist Jack Black expressed without a flinch of consideration, the shortest route for Legislative favors, a mathematical formula straight out bribery or a whore or two. Jack Black operated the Three Tit Salon and Gambling House, he figured curiosity of three tits, induced a surge towards a Legislative lure, he bragged freely, stonewalling congressional reform labor laws was his striving pursuit. Jack Black was for real and so was Leland Stanford pertaining to the Central Pacific Railroad who acquired the funds and Chines labor to build the western half of the great adventure. Thanks to Jack Black Central, and Pacific Railroad!

Rejection:

I summited a carton to the New Yorker publication that was never published, of an elderly Lobbyist holding a fist full of money, the Lobbyist was bent over the Senator's desk, his skin was drooping downward over his unscrupulous piercing eyes, his index finger was dissecting a bill for a particular passage of interest, the Senator was reaching for the loot, the punch line, where is my pork," a satire I labeled, "Is it graft or politics as usual," it was never published. If you think about it, the first Lobbyist exhumed an eerie odor of corruption. A Myth from Ode! A Garden called Eden, where a Snake peddler charmed the first legislator; it was the Midas fruit of excess.

Bickering without Possibilities:

Tension between Candidates is a bipartisan force of vengeance, that's reduced to a level of bickering, that's when Super Pac-is -a-cooking. The essential ingredient for cerebral proliferation is life's intoxication of unlimited character assassination. The greatest stigma to mankind, it's the wealthiest 1 % endeavor of self-indulgence. That's saying only a select influential few have a sense of identity; all others have no soul or the right of existence. Democratic or Republican bipartisan bickering is not the right to forgo a civic conscience of responsibility for all American's; the bottom line is the inalienable rights the Holly Grail and the last frontier of America.

Tax the wealthiest! Truman did, Ike topped him:

A realistic picture; a Billion income that's one thousand million; tax that fortunate individual 90% that affords a whopping 100 million take home pay. Ike did and achieved infrastructure and financial growth. The gift of arrogance, capital gains, Congressional leaders boldly state, with Legislative conviction! "Rich folks, won't spend money if you tax them!" Big Ticket Spenders! The top nine Banks have a consuming passion for acquisitions, ask B of A about Merrill Lynch and Countrywide, the major Plutocratic Executives use the term Luxury as a birth right, that's a 35,000 dollar room in Dubai, a Luxury Jet 35,000 daily, Yacht Charters 35,000 daily, or purchase a Yacht 35 Million, and it's all Tax deductible, if they are looking for something a little less expensive, Exotic cars, You can actually purchase a private Island or lease by the week, if your looking for an adventure into paradise, email / dturner@ millionairesconierge.com. According to our Legislators, if we tax the wealthy, they will stop spending money, that's like telling a Heroin abuser he's not an addict, Therefore the Government borrows from the poor folks Social Security, without "we the people" permission. The House Republican Representatives; signed a Lobbyist pledge, no new taxes for the Wealthiest 1%, they are on tax Welfare. BMW reported remarkable results for its ultra-expensive Rolls-Royce brand in the past six-months sold 970 Rolls-Royce starting at $400,000 U S dollars, they set a record they tripled the number sold in America a year ago. This ought to put a twist in your cerebral concept while snipe hunting with a glitter of 8.3% unemployed, while your holding onto that Crocker sack, observe the cost of living skyrocketing, the wealthy pay 103 dollars a pound for prime and you pay the tariff in taxes and they are exempt! Take solace those poor rich babies won't get delivery on their Rolls Royce till November of 2012.

91% and prospered:

In the fifties Ike taxed the rich 91% and America prospered, and Eisenhower brought the flowing ribbon of infrastructure into all 48 states, the Inner State Highway of prosper, our Education system was number "One debt free!" And our Corporations where in full pursuit of a great America, they promoted education! And fraud was a criminal act, with or without intent! Who the hell besides a five year old could sell a bag of crap that Moody's and S&P had no intent to defraud America, they should be downgraded to Fraudulent and prosecuted to the full intent. Its amazing Moody's downgraded Spain to Baa3 a half steep from junk status, that also includes 7 German Banking group and Austria's 3 biggest lenders. Cyprus downgraded to Ba3 two half steeps from junk status. Moody's a born again moralist without intent, converted for redemption. Try the interpretation without intent, if by chance you get arrested.

Citicorp enterprise:

An interesting non-fantasy, try a mythical highly implausible world, where Lobbyist cloister behind the Congressional halls of grievances, where deregulation set the rules of persuasion, where Lobbyist interpret the whims of Wall Street, the too big to Fail village, expunged the Congressional Glass Steagall Act from existence, a merger consolidated the ingredients of corruption, commercial banks, investment banks, Security firms and Insurance companies merged. Citicorp jumped the barrier, a Presidential waiver counteracted Constitutional law, and Citicorp merged with Travelers group insurance and became the birth of Citigroup, 1999 The Modernization act, effectuated the great American Real Estate triple A subprime mortgage rape, a Ponzi enterprise, that bankrupted Congress integrity, for whom the bells tolled S&P and Moody' s was in the thick of misrepresenting the truth, they swore it was without intent! The Lobbyist, 13,000 appeared in droves, abundance was their number, they steered the power five times greater, Ranking Staffers roamed the halls freely they became the rule makers, Lobbyist enhanced the ballet

of corruption, the dance of prolific spenders with a future into the
Lobbyist hereafter. A partisan majority extracted a magical
financial wonderment with President Clinton's approval, the
Financial Services Modernization Act, the bill encompassed pages
beyond pages not once did it mention, fraudulent opportunities for
the Conglomerates to merge; otherwise Watergate would have
been considered the first act of a Global tragedy! Chase in 2012
imploded to the tune of several billions and yet we refuse to
regulate. Every heard the term Frank Dodd!

The Ex Legislator:

With full realization, the lieges of Legislators, seeking
the Lobbyist million-dollar club depends on the ability to influence,
the numbers are staggering, 1 out of 3 Congressman or Senator
will serve the Conglomerate master faithfully. Congress must
explore the powerful present-day bearing within legislative
committees where financial opportunity dictates. Congress
including Staffers, must endure a curtailment period from lobbying,
for it will serve Congress' integrity that dedication is predicated to
serving the interest of "We the people," for excessive wealth is the
stepping stone of becoming a lobbyist; a two or three-year
sabbatical affords a proper playing field for all Americans, and not
the selected few.

Priority, Congress misplaced loyalty:

June 2012, 25 of our Military bravest committed
suicide, July 38 committed suicide they are dying without

recognition or appreciation, try justifying the too big to fail Banks foreclosure on active duty Military personnel, they sacrificed and served several combat tours, and came home to unemployment and foreclosure, shame on the Supreme Court interpreting freedom of speech afforded a group of misguided Ex patriots to degrade a hero's ultimate sacrifice, the living came home to an unappreciative America, when was the last time Congress made the ultimate sacrifice and honored our returning Veteran's with dignity, instead of foreclosure and unemployment! Rome forgot, and the Senate became indifferent. When excessive wealth takes priority over the welfare of our America fighting men, there will be no tomorrow! Think about the 56 men that signed the Declaration of Independence, their reward was liberty or death. 63 Veterans committed suicide in June and July their reward was indifference and foreclosure.

Corruption without intent:

In the twenty first Century plus ten there are in access of twelve thousand Lobbyist, the majority come from both Houses, not a single Lobbyist ever died over ethics, a slap on the wrist, that's like a bad hangover without intent; take a deep breath a shot of bourbon and swear it was without intent! Yet Wall Street exceeded in spending in excess of three billion! A point of clarification, I'm an Independent who believes ones political affiliation does not qualify a position of status, it's the obligation towards all Americans, commitment must be honored, not personal gratification. The majority of Americans have financially suffered in the twenty first century, except for the legislators with insider trading privileges, they have turned their immunity into gold, if you go into politics for financial attainment, and then hell and diarrhea should be your written reward.

The truth; all men are not created equal:

The Declaration of Independence, July 6, 1776 fifty-six men signed and pledged their lives fortunes and sacred honor, five signers, died at the hands of the British as traitors, Twelve had their homes burned to the ground, Nine fought and died in the Revolutionary War. They were lawyers, jurists, merchants, farmers and large plantation owners, and each where aware death was the penalty if captured. 87 years latter the Gettysburg Address, Four score and seven years ago our fathers brought forth on this continent a new nation, conceived in liberty and dedicated to the proposition that all men are created equal. "Of the people, by the people, for the people." Lincoln stated the world will little note; nor long remember what was said, Lincoln was right, profit before sacred honor, and yet we have our children sacrificing their lives fortunes and sacred honor for the proposition that all men are not created equal. Congress no longer has that sacred honor. It's time for Congressional Patriotism not the alternative! Ask Rome when you get to the hereafter.

The Budget and Pro Life, Political Narcissism:

A Federal budget Committee was in full debate, a perception of dispute detoured the menu of deficit, a runaway budget, without a mathematical value of balance, a twisted process of pork bickering, dismissed the deficit without scrutiny, transfixed activist Republican Pence a self-dictatorial anti-abortionist detoured the deficit from the boundary of importance. You got to be kidding!

The Federal Budget and anti-abortion played out like a Tennessee Williams novel, "a embryo on a hot tin roof!" tension erupted, stage left, Republican Pence, a self determined anti-abortion activist grappled the vibrational disdain of, "funding abortion," a wince enhanced a spastic curled lip, the budget deficit dispensed the bellow of Pence's dissatisfaction, plagued eyes clutched an uncontrollable agitation, "I don't apologize for it!" Pence tilted to a vocal rendition, "tax funding abortion," It was perpetuated by CNN Newscaster Bingham Thomas' verbal perspective pertaining to non conservative Pence, "Pence is an Idiot!"

Unbeknown Bingham verbally asserted his insightful opinion, viva an open mike, "that fool Pence has no earthly conformation that tax payers are financially supporting abortion, what an opportunistic idiot!" Pence reciprocated, to a shattering rendition of King Lear's tragedy, wrath cantankerous to a crusty, "go to hell! And you pay attention! I'm pro-life! I don't apologize for it, I'll shut down the government before funding a dollar for abortion!" Somehow I'm convinced Pence should consider anti-abortion and pro-life be confined to individual State legislation, but let's follow the plot, and if we are lucky we can bypass birth control legislation for an insightful importance the deficit.

The budget and the unknown:

Conservatively right, the stage shifts President Obama courtly in a Presidential manor states, "let's make a deal," tension enhances the partisan zone of intensity, deliberation wiggles and waggles towards a pork cookout, the magical sum of the unknown, they where definite about budget cuts, that sounds profoundly suspicious to expedite, when the annual reduction of deficit hung below a Trillion dollars, that's when the planet of Waco mathematics marked the deficit! The 2012 to 2021 Congressional budget a factor without a probability, the Management and budget OMB the Executive and Legislative branch had no concept of reality, for balancing a Budget deficit. That's like giving an addict a Visa card with unlimited credit. Can you say trillions without spilling it?

A little pork, and a little less Education:

How in God's name! Do you educate selectively by the weight of financial status, when Congress considers $522,000 Pork for blueberry disease over Education, while Congress cuts endowment programs and degrade Teachers with the stigma of less than, the Pell grants for college students, the Peace Corps and the National Endowment for the Arts. Social studies are no longer integrated into the Education system of our children, yet I was taught in elementary school that character traits of responsibility cultivated a civic virtue of community, it's no longer a concern towards civic orientation the economy shifted into the unholy grail, flip flopping credibility into oblivion. Please explain why Congress deserves a pay raise over Teachers, when in truth the majority of Legislators require a calculator, the ego-tripping truth, the American Voter needs only a lever to make change in their Legislators!

A Political statement, where is the pork!

Mr. Boehner House Majority leader stated, "We need to reduce the number of spending earmarks, but!" As he paused, a sense of adjustment was forth coming, "I don't know that it's appropriate to eliminate all of them." The term," but!" However goes a long way in both Houses?

Mr. Boehner when confronted in response to Jack Abramoff comment about curbing graft, Mr. Boehner responded, venturing cautiously into compromise, "I would favor more disclosure of dealings with lobbyists, but do not seek complete bans on travel or earmarks." In truth, when scandals achieve news worthy, Congress reacts with double talk diplomacy, thirty days later, nobody knows what the hell you are talking about."

George Bernard Shaw:

"Capitalism has destroyed our belief in any effective power but that of self-interest backed by force." I agree the Lobbyist system is that force!

Food for thought!

President Obama expresses a partisan possibility, "If we cut 80 billion from Higher Education over the next ten years, that's a measly 8 billion yearly! Texas dropout rate rose above the 50% mark. Pork less kosher than earmarks, spending in 2010 16.5 billion! That's spending millions in Pork for a Quail's sex life, is not educational, try perverted! President Obama you have another four years to get it right! Think before you speechify the written words of idiots even if they are cleaver Democrats. Try 700,000 and above for tax increase, Presidents of the past, have proven it works!

2012 try not walking on the stupid side:

CTE has an enormous, impact on students, school systems and our ability to prosper as a nation. The Administration's budget proposal was a slight reduction of $264 million in funding, which excluded the option of literacy. Education a nation's ability to survive and prosper, Now 52.7 Billion in foreign Military assistance, Korea a prosper country contributed, diddlysquat! CTE takes the bullet, a 14 % reduction; explain a trillion in Student Loan debt that enhances the deficit mark of an Education or Social Security, when you fund a gorilla with a feces problem. The economy will go belly up! Now if you tax the wealthiest 1% a realistic 90%, it should be considered a good start. Hell that 1% of wealthy folks will work twice as hard; they are addicted to the green stuff! It's time to take back our Country, a campaign promise that must be fulfilled, reform the tax code and let the Plutocrats pay their fair share. I believe in the first amendment for "We the people", I don't adhere to graft, fraud, pork, earmarks or influence peddling for the select few. I do believe in prosecuting the guilty! The problem we would have to close down Wall Street and half of Congress.

1956 America's upswing:

Elvis Presley's 'Heartbreak Hotel hits gold, Israel invades Suez Canal and Nasser was removed the year 1956. A new vocabulary appeared on the horizon, brainstorming, brinkmanship, Industrial Park and Tranquilizer, Ford Motor had an inspiration, "They'll know you've arrived when you drive up in an Edsel," The ten Commandments, around the world in eighty days, What's left in the Twenty First Century, Greed Mongers! Say goodbye America for 1% rains supreme.

Andrew Jackson in 1835 balanced the Budget, National Bank's Biddle told President Jackson to back off, or he would destroy Jackson's Presidency, Jackson informed Biddle he would simply kill him, he did it without a duel, Jackson terminated Nicholas Biddle ability to function, Jackson simply removed National Bank's gold and silver reserve. Biddle should have not threatened Jackson. A Senator remarked that Jackson fought so many duels, "13 to be exact" that every time he stood up he rattled like marbles from the lead. He also did threaten to hang Vice President John C. Calhoun from a tree. 1832 Vice President John C. Calhoun resigned, Jackson didn't believe in filibustering.

Congress over Education:

Embark upon a generation once cherished, 1950s technology, research and development created intellectual capital an indispensable marquee for modernization, technological effort remained the exclusive preserve of American throughout 1950s and 1960s. High School Graduates one out of three interred Collage; it was the dawn of indispensable growth for America. 2012 we have a Trillion dollar Student Loan the death count of education affordability, without title of respect, teachers are underpaid; tuition and fees have escalated above the 20% mark in 2012, Public Universities cost factor starts at $18,500 to $21,000, Harvard 100,000 plus for Education affordable to a select few. In broad daylight GE professes proudly, billions spent for GE's tax welfare, wriggled with devious loopholes paid not a single Tax dollar for America. That's like saying; I got great news! I indebted my neighborhood children from attaining an Education into a wonderful world of poverty, but the good news; I have moved to China, tax-free into the child labor hereafter! Greed outranks future dignity and the American educational system, what the hell happened to Washington crossing the Delaware; it's called Wall Streets bottom line. A mathematical note of interest, increase Educational excellence by 20% and America will financially prosper in less than 15 years, China understands that Mathematical formula, new horizons to conquer, for skilled and cerebral productivity, They have one billion 300 million people, and according to their educational growth by 2029 they will have purchased America without firing a single shot. And our wealthiest 1% will be living in Dubai or China. They built a bridge in China and shipped it to Oakland USA, lock stock and inferior steel. Congress has taken a pledge no new tax, that's saying 280 million Americans should learn to suck it up! The price of the poor mans peanut butter increased 22%!

Academia starts at day care!

China's National Academia starts at Day Care, children speak English proficiently and knowledgeable of American culture. The numbers are staggering 128,000 of the brightest Chines students are studying in our Universities, 30 % increase excelled in the year 2012, China will triple in 2013 output. China's number one subsidy, Education and most profitable undertaking. We have subsidized the wealthiest of Conglomerates, beyond the realm of sanity. Congress needs to lock the revolving door on their illiteracy and stop giving our taxpayer dollars away to Wall Street, Tax the wealthy 1% on a proper financial ratio 90%. It's simple let's subsidize, our Education System and in 15 years America will be in the black. Our Legislative trendsetters are spouting off like five year olds with two nickels and a bag of marble mentality, "easily bought easily corrupted". Our Legislators need to take a course! "We the people!" We are in a Global Universe of competition, Education, infrastructure for the 21st Century, and Outer Space is the only living frontier left. Oh I forgot we shut that program down, and Russia said, "what was it called, on yeah! Sputnik."

2012 China No 1 in Education, America 30th:

President Obama was misinformed, we don't rank

second; globally we rank 30th in the aspect of our Educational system, except for Student loans indebtedness; we hit the Mark of denial. A reality check, China ranks globally first in Math, Science and Reading, you asked! America ranks 30th in math, Science we have no bragging rights we rank 20th and reading, I can't believe we are 17th, T. S. Eliot the evolution of an artistic genius into the 21st century. This charm of vacant lots! The helpless fields that lay Sinister, sterile, and blind. I embraced T.S Eliot's poem into a future prose of America the dying egoist, Eliot was clairvoyant in his perception of a corrupt society, Entreat the eye and rack the mind, as our deficit grows, with ashes and tins in piles as the future of America declines, without glitter of excellence, for greed became the criers message, for Education sterile less than, Shattered bricks and tiles, and the debris of a city, will linger, without the educated. On February 11th, Rep. Hal Rogers, Chair of the House Appropriations Committee, introduced a "New Bill" reducing funding for Educational programs. T. S. Eliot's insightful image, I saw their lives curl upward like a wave and break. And after all it had not broken. Wall Street showed no respect of attitude, it might have broken even across the grave, and yet our Educators excel without position of title, for Congress became the menu of financial lessening, of tendencies unknown and questions never spoken. Behind close doors was the gap of obligation, a trillion for Pork! Illiteracy became the lament of deficit. Hal Rogers Chair of the House Appropriations Committee, stated, that a reduction of 10%, allowed those unsung hero's to maintain their position as Educators; yet they paid their fair share of taxes, without a single loophole to deduct, with a student loan attached. The Legislative arena of affluent afforded GE tax-free status with billions hoarded off shore. A thought, pork for understanding a Quail's sex life, that's not kosher, please enlighten the House Appropriations Committee, the definition of politically corrupt is illiteracy. In the aftermath of December 7,1941 our only initiative was survival, we took the task at hand for we where 100 % America. And we taxed the Wealthy and they prospered. And we honored openly with tears for our fallen hero's

Pork for 2012 will exceed the promise:

Life deprived between ignorance and extinction, a perimeter without vision! Mr. President Education was America's path of National Pride, for the Universe holds the last untold frontier for America to evolve. Two decades and the world should have asked why didn't Congress eliminate earmarks, pork and subsidies back in 2012 when the deficit was in full bloom, America's last true frontier Education. Private enterprise will not concur, for greed belongs to a select few, its called Super Pac self-indulgence without a future!

Deficit an astonishing lack of insight:

Iraq exceeded the Trillion-dollar expenditure. Afghanistan now exceeds 60 billion and Congress funds Pork and Earmarks for the sex life of Quail, yet not one red cent increased for Education! America's palette an Old Academy rendering from 1802, of promise and hope, a frontier where devoted patriots tempered by attainment was conceived. West Point the first Military Academy founded by Congress march 16, 1802 education the theory of military excellence. A rill of grandeur that sat upon unknown horizon of infinite dreams, for fortune yet not conceived, yet hollow the future without a frontier to ascend, the genesis of discovery. February 1, 2003 Shuttle Columbia was scheduled to touch down at Kennedy Space Center, within fifteen minuets disaster, a legacy to Rick D. Husband, William C. McCool, David Brown, Laurel Blair Salton Clark, Michael P. Anderson, Ilan Ramon, and Kalpana Chawla. The final line of the rendering, "Old Academy," for time forged its quondam of heroic patriots. Yet it was the last frontier of America's pride of attainment; it's been replaced with Wall Streets billion dollar club for the select few!

God the Genesis Of Discovery:

President Thomas Jefferson wrote, "The God who gave us life gave us liberty at the same time" and asked 'Can the liberties of a nation be secure when we have removed a conviction that these liberties are not of God?" 2012 the debate if God is Constitutional! First things first, Congress must comprehend the Universe does exist! The Constitution might not! If both Houses conceive being elected is the platform to a Lobbyist fortune! The facts, fifty present convert and Congress talks about a two or three-year restriction before becoming a lobbyist, the reality hell will freeze over first.

The world is a stage, but the play is badly cast:

Oscar Wilde comment on the colonies, America is the Country that went from barbarism to decadence without civilization in between. Try fraud for a bonus!

I envisioned the peers of the realm from my youth; with Title of Senator and Congressman transcend the breath and aspiration of Constitutional freedom, "we the people," not the Lobbyist of arbitration, for in the 21 Century they serve the Plutocratic masters of privilege, a quest without documentation or constitutional purpose. The Lobbyist bearing set forth its masters unwavering resolute of domination. A trancelike undertow the gathering of wheelers and dealers, rendered a flavor was amiss, a magical affirmation of Political corruption, rang the amendment of grievance, sculptured a Lobbyist deception for an Individual fancy, represented in human form. Like spectators the scavengers feast on Trillions off shore, while 8.3 % of Americans unemployed on our shores.

An Oscar Wilde quote, "Only dull people are brilliant at breakfast." That's why Lobbyist, show up at brunch. Oscar Wilde was sentenced to two years for being a homosexual, it was the law of morality, when released, he was penniless, rejected and died in Paris, at the age of 46. His genius outlived the political moral bigots of their day.

Privileged, requires a fable and a Lobbyist:

The day of the Lobbyist! Brought forth the Conglomerates fable, the marginal-productivity theory!" The 1%, by the 1% for the 1 %, they pledge upon every thing sacred, with fleece of breath, they professed the higher the income, the higher the productivity, financial disbursement was afforded the affluent, which these demigods, preach upon the holly grail, privileged opulence walks on the blind side of humanity. For their lies the bleached-bones of the majority, for they have vanished without a whimper or a vote, just the wisp of the privileged, from a place called Wall Street!

A Repast, tax deductible, not charitable:

$100 billion yearly for the tax privileged, Wall Street traders and the super wealthy deduct $1,000 for a charitable repast, and brag of their superior social life style and nobody in Congress considers that objectionable. The federal government has allowed the Tax payer to be fleeced, hoodwinked, defrauded, gulled and stiffed by the wealthy in excess of $100 billion for charitable events that have an openhanded value, one of self-indulgence. Considered an intellectual formula, 100 billion for Education; that becomes an effective trickle down marginal-productivity theory. Instead of Congress having a key to insider trading, when 8.3 Americans are unemployed, and the great American dream, get wealthy and to hell with your heritage! No American should be Homeless, hungry, or without Medical assistance, that's not socialism, that's just giving a damn about your American family before excess!

A reality check!

I observed a vogue creature of extreme vulgar wealth,

flaunting an original creation of self-importance, as she expressed her worldly stature of excess, it was what she considered, "the Connoisseur Delight known as the, Sumptuous Repast of Accomplishment", on National Television to a self absorbed glee of onlookers as if she had been honored with the Pulitzer Prize. For awe was in full bloom on national TV, she expressed that she and two of her friends paid a thousand dollars each for breakfast; they consumed a variety of exotic protein with gold shavings sprinkled over a spotted quail egg. What the hell, if several million kids go to bed without a spotted Quail egg hungry; that's the insanity of a Plutocratic ego massaging its stature of financial status without a concern, that 8.3 % unemployed have become void of existence, there are 40,000l in New York City the home of Wall Street, and to be bothered with their Social needs, that's inconsiderate on the part of the unemployed and homeless. The mark of justification, "I have that special friend," definition that's somebody you can't name and has never been to your home, correction as a maid yes, as a guest hell no!

A time before the Lobbyist bought Capital Hill:

Back in 1936 the sky was lucid beyond the heavens, the Mississippi River was indisputable three-dimensional crystal clear and drinking water was consumed right out of the garden hose. Water was free and coffee was a nickel with unlimited refills, the beach was sandy white as the early morning exposed crustaceans beneath the sand as the incoming tide exposed them by the cardinal number of an immeasurable crest, and shell-life left its trail of movement; the beach sixty years later became the regime that simply perished for the bottom line, mercury, oil and profit.

The Constitution never indicated the House or the Senate was above the law yet a select few, have taken upon themselves behind close doors, the recipients of arrogance flaunting billions for anti-legislation and lucrative futures; Big Oil anti-environmental Lobbyist contributed billions, they hoodwinked and deferred the Freedom of Information Act. The State Department, refused disclosure between Congress and the anti-environmental Lobbyist, proclaiming confidentiality was to protect our natural resources. From Chesapeake Bay, to the Gulf of Mexico, count the countless dead streams and polluted rivers, for they exclude the excessive discard of nutrients, bacteria, mercury, oil slush, toxic chemical dumping, sediment and pesticides, "We don't have a Congress or legislation protecting our natural resources, the polluters are being subsidized billions as the oil spills into the gulf, if you can smell it, then you can spell Ex Senator and Congressmen anti-environmental Lobbyist. The Environmental Protection Agency will be cut 1.6 billion; according to their ability to protect the environment, they must have only two employees and one brings a pillow to work, we have increased subsidies spending to 35.5 billion dollars. Simplot have you tried the two headed fried fish on a bun of toxic nutrients, yum, yum! The fish have mutated, JR Simplot Co. according to the EPA have not exceeded the limits for humans to glow in the dark.

Global Conglomerate privileged and subsidized!

Can you say, "four dollars and nine tenth cent into oblivion?" Oil Subsidies, created a point of interest; President Obama responded with a request, for Congress to end Oil Subsidies, House Speaker, Boehner, e-mailed the President citing an analysis by the Congressional Research Service, ending subsidies would drive oil and natural gas prices to escalate. Was that a threat or a promise! Guess what? Gas prices are escalating! Trillions of dollars sit offshore avoiding taxation. The absolute certainty, it's broken, therefore fix it! Oil informed the world; billions in profits for the forth quarter, the Lobbyist are patient for that magical marker the trillion-dollar mark! The certitude, that created the phantom of invisible Trillions evolved into a global Market." It will remain an invisible deficit until the IRS tax code introduces a Global bilateral Tax covenant, remove double taxation, and prosecute tax evasion, promote the foreign direct investment (FDI) through a lower effective tax rate. At present Congress is listening to a thousand independent Lobbyists, with a thousand independent idiosyncratic symbols of individual tax grievances. Introduce a Global Tax format for the majority, and bring America's capital back to our shores. A fact, Wall Street Lobbyist bolster a fortified mentality to increase jobs, in fact their bottom line, indicates just off shore, not in the USA! Prof China's Market replaces five American jobs hourly and the American Conglomerate acquires 100 child labors.

Congress and Global:

General Electric paid no taxes, and bragged of its exploit of ascendancy; yet they are safeguarded by the

Constitution, sure as the eagle soars! The Global GE is no longer an American kindred spirit. ExxonMobil's tax rate 0.4, while they acquired billions in subsidies, plus collected a $156 million rebate, and demanded additional tax relief, the bottom line! Profit before honoring responsibility to keep America beautiful. Bank of America's tax refund was $1.9 billion, plus billions in bailout, to hell with our next generation for we will afford our children the privilege of being homeless, or a country to be enslaved by the Plutocrats whims. Goldman Sachs in 2008 paid 1.1 percent of taxes, its profit $2.3 billion and for the past five years received billions from the Federal Reserve. Wall Street has the Golden key to the revolving door, while Schools and Teachers pay the price of the deficit. Carnival Cruise Lines made in access of $11 billion in profits, tax rate 1.1 percent, the Cruise Line Industry Association gave the lobbying firm Alcalde and Fay in excess of a million, and spent a couple million on lobbying Congress. Yet Congress bypass the reality that twelve miles of Southern California they dump hundred of thousands of gallons of virus infected feces, that's a profitable way to look at the bottom line, crap on America and feed the crab population, they love infected gourmet, and another Congressman becomes a Lobbyist. Valero Energy, the 25th largest company in America earned $168 billion last year and had the right Lobbyist an Ex Senator, and collected a 157 million dollar tax refund, their tax rate 4.2%, subsidies are a blessing for the bottom line, especially if you have a profitable forth quarter. Chesapeake Energy tax rate was a whooping zero%! A single comment, you got to be kidding! The US Federal Income Tax Rate for these 42 US Big Oil Corps for the past 3 years combined, was a meager 4.9%. It's time that both Congress and the Senate advocate a political theory, socialism should be a periodical for the less fortunate in a democracy of Capitalism, its the kindred spirit of caring that has kept America strong and prosper. Congress ought to give it a try! And support our Country, for the less fortunate usually are the ones dying for their Country, and they are not subsidized, yet foreclosure became a warriors stigma for serving and dying for his country.

Evolution and Globalization:

The 'expenditures of Globalization, known as the 10 giant loopholes cost the government $125.6 billion last year, that's what came into the daylight.

Globalization, Conglomerate Lobbyist mind set, have adopted an off shore mentality, cheap labor, eliminate paying taxes. According to GE the oppressive tax regime they have circumvented by crossing national borders lock stock and X ray barrel into a Tax free, China.

Tax incentive dispense with American Labor:

Pharmaceutical Pfizer a mythical Globalized Individual, first and most important dispensed with over 59,000 jobs, while Pfizer including additional off shore Pharmaceutical companies are coercing Congress with an arm-twisting influence of substantial financial leverage of persuasion, it's off shore billion parked overseas. Seven years ago Congress declared a tax holiday! They celebrated Congress decreased Pfizer tax burden from 35 percent to 5 percent, an immunity of $85 billion from federal taxes, Pfizer repatriated, the cost to American tax payers

$300 billion and Congress; did not envision the globalization light bulb was flickering, cheap labor and pretax profit. Pfizer and several thousand other Conglomerates will not hire American Employees. Congress must enact a Global Conglomerate bilateral Tax covenant, to eliminate double taxation, stimulate the FDI through an effective tax rate, an incentive for American jobs. Tax incentive procures taxable profit and jobs, the mark of being an American embrace your obligation and your fair share of taxes, if we ask our youth to die for our freedom, then we have the right for Congress to demand America first.

Corporate Welfare, Global:

The unemployed numbers increase monthly; no matter Democrat or Republican Politicians they absolved their dedication, to represent "we the people!" To date Congress serves the plutocratic Global Lobbyist elite. Corporative Global Welfare from a mathematical formula expedites the decline of American work force, GE Healthcare acquired Clarient, a worldwide leader in Cancer diagnostic, GE Oil & Gas acquired Wellstream Holdings operations. GE Global Energy acquired Dresser, Inc. for 3 billion. GE Electric Co. acquired five new partnerships within China totaling in excess of 2 billion in technology and research, GE is competing with U.S. based Boeing, I swear, Chief Executive Officer Jeffrey Immelt was proud to announce 1,000 new jobs for China. I have a question, how in hell did Jeffrey Immelt become the head of President Obama's council on Jobs and Competitiveness. Jeffrey Immelt informed the world, China the world's fastest-growing aviation market, energy, transportation, health care and financial services, had committed 2 billion for China's economy. GE the parent Co. of NBC received 24.9 Million in Stimulus funds, reduced their U.S. employees by 18,000 in 2009. G.E. a $600 billion enterprise generated $150 billion in revenue and $12 billion in profit last year, they didn't pay a single dollar in Taxes, GE bragged not one red cent for Taxes."

Try fixing the problem:

Globalization has become the Twenty First Century supplemented labor force a clandestine enterprise of Tax loopholes and billions undeclared profit. It's the evolution of revision, QRT Tax = Flat Tax. The quantitative ratio tax QRT would revolutionize the tax system. Fiscal Income simplification tax, the ratio of working population and individual income a flat tax measured by ratio of Wages, Salaries, Pensions, less Personal Allowance. The low-income citizens a reduced share of the tax ratio therefore the economy prospers, tax revenues grow, affording increase entrepreneurial incentive in risk taking. A woodenhead halfwit can find fault, except Congress can't find a solution.

Can you spell Op's?

Hay guess what? "Do you remember BP's Gulf Oil mishap, an international demonstration of arrogance to the environment, it has become a 9.9 billion dollar oil spill compensation package for BP. The master plan, BP intends to milk $9.9 billion from the United States Tax payers based on a

32.2 billion uncertified accounting. President Obama insisted BP would soak up the out-and-out expenditure of their environmental infamy, the sludge of I don't give a damn, has crippled, maimed and mutilated the environment, human lives and wildlife, yet BP announced it will claim $9.9 billion in U.S. tax credits, plus bonus for the competent executives of spin. The federal government's general fund will be 9.9 billion less. We have observed BP say op's that's not all that bad.

You got to be kidding!

Nuclear power plants and fuel cycle facilities in all United States Regions; exceed the number one hundred and still counting. The 10 highest risk nuclear power outlets, they occupy unusual sites, thanks to the Lobbyist wisdom we placed them on Earthquake faults, take your pick [NY, MA, TN, PA, CA, VA, SC.] Op's who would have ever conceived the tragedy or the estimated devastation to Japan in 2011. It gives thought to Alex Flint Lobbyists for the nuclear energy industry, I'd venture that Alex was bellowing into the atmosphere, reassuring members of Congress the crisis in Japan was a separate incident from our superior systems. Somebody should have asked him, where are we dumping our nuclear waste, into the Ocean it's designated Sea disposal Implementation, Belgium, France, Federal Republic of Germany, Italy, Japan, Netherlands, Russia, South Korea, Switzerland, UK and the USA. It's embracing how the Plutocratic conglomerates have outright purchased our demise for profit; they spent billions on Legislatives to convince the American public that Mr. Smith goes to Washington to represent, we the people, but the problem, he now owes 300 million to the Plutocrat of his choice. We the people have the right to petition government for a redress of grievances; "You got to be kidding, do you have a lobbyist!"

The 1% Privileged Individual:

I will refer to the Lobbyist as the Plutocratic fraternities influence peddlers with muscle, for they represent the Privileged 1% and they alone consumes 42.9 % of the financial wealth, the next 19% are "the buffer and the determined wannabes" they consume 51%, that leaves the majority of American's, that's the other 80 % of us, we receive 7% of the scraps. The Supreme Court in a majority session, stipulated under the fourteen amendment a Company, has been labeled an Individual, the bottom line, the fourteen amendment stipulates, it will not deprive any person of life, liberty, or property, without due process of law; nor deny to any person within its jurisdiction the equal protection of the laws. Therefore accordingly an Individual who pays personal tax is a marginal factor not a Corporation, somehow the Supreme Court in its wisdom deemed a system of documents, deeds, contracts, instruments of Corporation a covenant of commitment between profit and loss, with a singular isolated term "Individual" that's an Individual adjective with a mathematical value of 1. General Electric, the "person" acquired a tax free immunity, by investing billions in China, GE healthcare unit the X-ray for the past 115 years was an American based business, it was transported lock stock and barrel to Beijing China, why you ask? Cheap labor and excess profit and tax-free status and no passport required for GE the "person" returning to America! That "person" bypassed an obligation to America and heritage, and bragged about it! I have a name for GE and it's not an individual or human! Oh yeah in 2008 GE the "person" cried directly to the Secretary of State Hank for financial assistance from the hording banks.

A day into the future:

The day November 7th 2026, two cycle of deregulation devoured the liquidity without bearing or redemption of we the people, Wall Street Lobbyist consumed without recoil of responsibility; ravenous eclipsed a shattering prose of silence, across flowing lines marked the mortal pang of declining stocks; securities bearish, red in numbers 27 Trillion tilted without a trace of stimulus. "Violence shakes my dreams, like rapture breaking on the mind," Stanley Kunitz Pulitzer-winning Poet when asked about his poem responded, "A poem comes in the form of a blessing or not, like rapture breaking on the mind." As I continued to read from Kunitz poem I envisioned a predatory villain of Capitalism without morality of vision; what lingered, was not salvation for the majority, "As Scholars dungeoned in an ignorant age, tended the embers of the Trojan fire. Cities shall suffer siege and some shall fall,"

I conceive the scholars shall echo Kunitz legacy, from candor to prophet, the celestial fraught was not rebuffed ungracious neither abrupt, without justification nor apologetic sized the deficit, without a whisper or a musty reminder, survival was transient at best. Political resentment the prevalent accuser with spice of famine prevailed the gambit, for the privileged few; rode the hordes of tormented masses, a stench of contempt nightly scribed it flare of graffiti, scared with illicit belligerence superiority perished without deliberation held the stench of demise, "the Day of the Lobbyist", lingered a fraudulent wasp of the Godless nexus, relinquished its dominion, for "we the people," no longer existed. Hunger was all that remained! Food for thought!

When Wall Street ruled, Déjà vu, Black Tuesday:

My first thought, why in daylight saving time, do we afford Wall Street to override an intellectual process of survival; time and time again we afford the Demigods of self-indulgence to deregulate.

The Dream:

President Herbert Hoover's inauguration speech in March of 1929, the great American dream, "Given the chance to go forward with the policies of the last eight years, we shall soon with the help of God, be in sight of the day when poverty will be banished from this nation. We the people; will regulate the American ideals of individualism and self-reliance." And disaster loomed behind close doors. From History's point of view, the myth of the three blind mice, Hoover was listening to Wall Streets fraudulent hype, " the economy will only grow if we deregulate, in 1998 William Jefferson Clinton stated, " the economy will only grow if we deregulate."

Madoff asked, "Can you do that!"

The Down Jones Industrial that year in 1929 was soaring skyward, without a quiver of hesitation, affluence excelled an inspirational plate of greed, and Wall Street was sizzling in its duplicitous opulence. September 3rd Black Tuesday, a blip faltered, to a nebulous percent, Bullish bellowed a bearish decline, as stocks liquidated assets far beyond peril, Down Jones faltered to a hush death spiral, death imploded violently into oblivion, Wall Street plummeted from prosperity without a sense of finality, Banks ceased, darkness immersed without breath or compassion into insolvency, unemployment vacillated without a figure of accuracy, political bickering signified default for America. All that is valuable in human society depends upon the opportunity for development accorded the individual. "Quote by Albert Einstein."

The 7th President and Rufus:

Andrew Jackson said, "You must pay the price if you wish to secure the blessing. Every good citizen makes his country's honor his own, and cherishes it not only as precious, but also as sacred. He is willing to risk his life in its defense and its conscious that he gains protection while he gives it." I shook the hand right out of Confederate History; his name was Rufus! The year was 1937.

The day Johnny Reb impacted my life:

July 4, 1937, I was seven and about a hand shake away from a living breathing Confederate soldier, Rufus Hannibal Taylor, I was confronted by the embodiment of Heroic nobility from a thousand years past, I was transfixed with a sense of wonderment, beyond grip seized by mortal concept, totally oblivious in manner I had nonchalantly page and chapter transcended the twilight zone, older than Methuselah was Rufus Hannibal Taylor. I gawked without civil thought; reality engraved the leaf of Pickett's charge, embedded bygones echoed the cutting stone of the dead. Rufus Hannibal Taylor reached the nostalgic pages a drift from yore, summoned by a single finger I was transfixed without intent, bewitched a thousand thoughts an uncanny mirage of a mythical bygone transmuted a child's imagination, delusion fluctuated back and forth, a solvent thought etched my silent trance one step then a second to reflect, "god he ought to be dead", a remaining step untouchable, I was eyeball to eye ball absent of recall, the aura transfixed his existence, Johnny Reb himself, sitting frozen beyond yesterday, a hat half cocked both hands clasped an old crocked hickory cane as if he had just fought his last battle, leather worn skin whispered its past without an inkling, my finger reached out as if that alone, afforded my gateway to a childish thought to inquire, "Sir did you ever see anybody killed?" as if motion didn't exist, a grating breath seemed to glide his bidding, "The truth son," held a silent pause, a slight tilt tweaked a fixed expression, Rufus slowly adjusted that old confederate cap, I recalled a coy simper, with a click of his mouth, I became the forbearer of ninety some years, he ventured bygone memories of times past, "Son, I never had the honor to meet death personally, but that there self-evident thing, that Robert E. Lee was talking about, how all men where created equal to their individual beliefs, they sure enough in that Civil war died equal. Those them their Presidents John Adams and Thomas Jefferson who put pen to that Declaration, did you know, both them their Presidents died on that July fourth day in 1826 of natural causes. Yeah my paw said they didn't really like each other." With a slight scowl my hand he touched, his hair was frizzled sort of grayish right down to his shoulders, his mustache was massive stained from tobacco juice truly impressive, his medals clinched tightly to his Confederate weather beaten uniform, dried blood embellished stains of his last battle near New Hope church outside Marietta Georgia, he said that it was his last battle. I was mesmerized there I stood next to a living reb from1864 the words held me spell bound as he reflected a magical past drifting back into that final chapter and time, "Yeah it had ah been a raining for eleven straight days, that there day I got myself shot it had done stopped raining, it was that there twelfth day," with a slight sense of awe, I envisioned a mud soaked road wagons buried to their axles, for stench of defeat was in his eyes, scribed on his bearing of manner, it was his final bugle call. I asked my Father afterwards, "I just wondering dad, do you think Rufus wears that uniform all the time or only on special occasions?"

"Hell Son," My father responded with an all-knowing smirk, as if the answer was written in stone, "they will bury Rufus in that uniform, that's a badge of pride he wears every day of his life, the Rebel Yell! Will be his final thought as he passes into the ages with all his memories."

In my day of days, I voyaged by crystal radio beyond reality into WW11. The wounded veterans came forth from battle, they the ultimate warriors, anguish beyond inspire, a blind marine crying, his brother marines needed him, and he let them down, the true value Patriotism, today we have Veterans homeless and jobless who served two and three tours in Iraq. And Congress is concerned if we tax our wealthiest it will bring America financially to its knees. A message to Congress when America was prosperous we taxed the wealthy 91% and they worked twice as hard and prospered. We where number one in Education and nobody earned a billion dollars for betting against America losing!

Lobbyist and the first amendment:

In 1937 Dracula was the rage and Bela Lugosi's famous one liner "I'll drink your blood," that creative line was afforded a hundred year shelf life along with Twinkies, that's just about the total sum of what will survive the twenty first century. The Wall Street obligation to America; has become Corporative wealth beyond humanity and infinity. The Lobbyist, the liege of Persuasion, faithfully serve their Plutocratic masters, a single determination alter, influence and lure the Legislators and Government officials into a single minded illusion Deregulation serves American interest, except Congress and deregulation serves its 1% Overlord masters intemperance, we are 17 in education, and 210 million Americans are 120 day from being homeless, our debt to China exceeds the point of no return. And Congress believes 210 million Americans are retarded, Our greatest growth in the twenty century we taxed the wealthy 90% and we prospered, Today the great Myth, welfare for the wealthy is our only form of survival.

Hold Sway God's first choice:

A tribute, Susan B. Anthony, "We can no more deny forever the right of self-government to one-half of our people, than we could keep them forever in bondage. Come it will, and I believe within a generation for "Failure is impossible!" Women were given the vote on August 26, 1920, it occurred fourteen years after Susan B. Anthony's death. Mitt get a life, it's not what you can do for Women! It's what Women can do for America! Only a women gives life to a generation, a man's responsibility, have respect for God's first choice! Congress can no more deny forever the right of the Constitution" We the people."

1933 was an insightful time, on Capital hill:

June 25, a sunny lazy laid back day in 1933, sprawled out like an old hounds toil of sweltering yesterday, a half stifled wheeze awaiting a sparse twitch for tomorrows breeze, far above that old hounds imposing reach, swaying to an ungratifying annoyance of displeasure, a verbose jaybird in a heckling delight chattered aggressively its feathered intensity, exacerbated that old hounds shiftless tranquility. The Senate in full debate, an electric fan half twirling to a pivotal squeal of collapse, drenched to swelter of discomfort, Senator Glass oblivious laid bare a savor of displeasure, an aristocratic curled upper lip staring bluntly towards a celling fan, his handkerchief was monogramed with perspiration, he spoke with manor of an orator's command, "I'm considering banning that foolish good for nothing dial phone," without thought Senator Glass paused, shifted so slightly as if expediency expressed a compromise of a cool breeze, with a waffling sneer of displeasure stated, "Mr. President, I personally will not be pestered, indulging myself with a fools gadget of dialing a circle, I shall retain my opinion God willing, regarding my manual telephone, although those good Senator's who desire to be pestered, for only they knows why! They should proclaim their distinction of achievement, partisan or not! All right, let's get with it!"

The scar of deregulation was without prosperity, an infinitive petition called for a directive to regulate Wall Streets financial services. Senator Glass and Senator Steagall had the insight along with the entire majority of Democrats, Republican and one Independent passed the Glass Steagall act of banking reforms the year 1933. "I don't have confidence in a Bank, that say's trust me, especially when the small print says different." A silent pause held hostage as Senator Glass snickered to a farcical conclusion, "Well, there's no doubt, what them Wall Street folks have gotten us into, Like I said, you got to watch them like a hawk or they will remove the socks off a dead man."

No truer words where spoken by President Andrew Jackson in 1833, the President was quoted in print, "it is to be regretted, that the rich and powerful, too often bend the acts of government, to their own selfish purposes. I have always been afraid of banks, if you aren't careful they will kill you."

The Glass Steagall act the Lobbyist Cliffhanger:

The saying, "If it's to good to be honest," then you must exceed the reality, there is a scoundrel waiting to adjudicate its fraudulent potential. The 73rd Congress in 1933 that consisted of 59 Democrats, the Republicans minority party comprised of 36 seats; and a single Farmer-Labor, a total 96 seats. They arbitrated, in a partisan mind-set concurred 96 to ought, the Glass Steagall act became the law, established the Federal Deposit Insurance Corporation [FDIC] that instituted banking reforms; designed to control speculation, and conflicts of interest, which was highly motivated by the Great Depression of 1929. The Majority of both houses in their moment of wisdom demanded Global Bank reform. Back in 1929 the term without intent, was not actable, fraud was a punishable crime. Sanity prevailed! The Glass Steagall Act brought forth a magical wand that held a mythical gift of inspiration with command of judgement. Congress stated with conviction freedom rings. A prose of mind and soul, if not regulated man will falter without intent in midstream, for glitter commands, before mortal man or politician.

Senator Steagall and Kipling's insightfulness:

Senator Steagall was confronted; outside the Willard Hotel Lobby by a rather aggressive reporter in passing; "Senator you know the Banks will repeal the Glass Steagall act before the ink dries." The Senator's stride missed a half step with a sneer of, say what! Tilted his head with a verbal tenacity confronted the reporter eyeball to eyeball, "if that transpires, "I tell you what! I won't be the one selling ice water on the street corner! I sort of go along with Kipling's poem about prosper, the Law of the Jungle, as old and as true as the sky; and the Wolf that shall keep it may prosper, but the Wolf that shall break it must die. And if you let them wolfs deregulate, the country will be consumed.

1936 morality was still in tact:

In 1936, Lucky Strike Cigarettes ran the great diet ad, smoke Lucky Strike's and lose weight. The FTC insisted that Lucky Strikes had made a small error in judgment and requested if they didn't want to be prosecuted to make a minor correction, and the new ad read, "Smoke instead of eating." Today you can observe a physical well defined Cowboy shirtless with an exposed six-pack [rectus abdominis,] as the caption proclaims in six foot letters, "It enhances my day, and I'm fulfilled." Morality on Wall Street has an unapproachable distinction that lies between, ethically whatever or ethically inaccurate but profitable. What the hell, a billion in bonus, helps avoid that 1% from reading the Want Ads.

41,000 applied, Banks approved three:

The archives of historical documents approved three, During the Great Depression mortgages decayed in a whisper of anguish, notification singular was boldly stamped, Foreclosure, deprived of compassion. President Herbert Hoover in 1932 enacted the first federal regulation, it was the Federal Home Loan Bank Act, designed to institute a credit reserve, it has a ring of familiarity, "41,000 homeowners applied, the Banks approved a whooping three applications," from the beginning of the Pharos, Banks hoard, in 1933 the Homeowners Loan act, awarded 770 million to the Thrift Banks, the 770 million was a treasure trove for the Banks and they flaunted their defiance, Congress in their wisdom in 1933 regulated the Banking Industry. The Glass Steagall act established the Federal Deposit Insurance Corporation eliminated Bank speculation, conflicts of interest and fraud. It required the Lobbyist special interest groups, sixty-six years, four months, and twenty-eight days, including billions to repeal the Glass Steagall act. And reclassify Corporative fraud not a criminal act, if without intent. Who the hell would have believed that without intent, transpired a criminal into a financial Demigod of renown!

Time had distinction and revision:

Al Capone had a gated residence at Alcatraz, with an ocean front view complements of the Government, a 11year airtight lease for participating in tax fraud, his culpability for killing a variety of associates somehow became a mute menu of dismissal, but Al Capone could not acquire that infamous Legislative without intent pardon, that was reserved for Wall Street and Legislators. The IRS had a strict policy, they didn't give a damn what your title or position, the bottom line, pay your tax's or its a gated residence. Unemployment had reached a whopping 20 percent, give or take a fluctuation of five or six percent according to the political party you asked back in the thirties, [trivia] a new car 450.00 dollars, with chrome trim and painted white walls it was a steal if you had a job and if not, the word steal would still apply, yet car manufacturers went belly-up, not a single government bailout. And yet during the great depression swarms of new Millionaires integrated into the background of the multitude of destitute, unemployment soared without compassion, that surpassed the peak of 25%, a compulsive hoard amassed a reservoir of Lobbyist, like scavengers devouring the remains of the American bleached bones. Yet, the American people had the fortitude of necessity, it became the birth of innovation, we the people, rolled up their sleeves and clawed back. 1999 the Lobbyist once again deregulated the American dream, and the 1% slowly consumed an additional 15% of the wealth. And America once again forgoes its past and deregulated.

1999 Deregulation:

An hour and a day latter K Street remove the safety net and turned it upside down, Wall Street invested 1.44 billion and the halls of Congress became the world of Lobbyist, and deregulations. That was the beginning of the end. The saying, "If it's to good to be true," the reality, there sits graft just around the corner waiting to acquire it! Two Chambers locked horns in a Jungle of legislative bickering for the pork roast, in July 1999, the infamous Gramm–Leach–Bliley Act a philosophical discussion for resurrection of Wall Street, the crier for prosperity, maneuvered its financial finger of paradise, four hogs of deregulation was the hunt. Wall Street Lobbyist ensured their position providing exclusion in the afterlife, that's like putting blinders on a horse then shooting him in public, and believing that nobody will observe the killing. Under the Bill of Rights, the fifth-amendment provided protection for privacy, the Lobbyist straw of inspiration was exclusion behind close doors, the Gramm–Leach–Bliley Act with blinders removed, nurtured an inspirational flare of fraudulent prosperity, President William Jefferson Clinton, introduced the Financial Services Modernization Act, Wall Street ran Bullish amuck and consolidated, mergers was the ingredient, commercial banks, investment banks, Security firms and Insurance companies the four hogs of deregulation. Citicorp was the first to propel the world of deregulation, they jumped the fence in 1998, they illegally merged with Travelers group to form the Conglomerate Citigroup, if you ask how's that possible! When it violated the Glass–Steagall Act, they had acquired in 1998 a waiver of approval, Citicorp negotiated behind close doors. Secretary of Treasury Robert Rubin, Lawrence Summers and Greenspan supported Citicorp's merger in 1998, a waiver legally finalized the fraudulent first steep, and they emerged as the magical Citigroup. Of course it was semi-not constitutional, but extremely profitable. Fraud without intent that's an oxymoron, or as Congress interprets intent; that accordingly by financial inducement becomes a waiver of certitude righteously acceptable. Then you have Insider Trading for Congress, you and I would be wearing prison stripes. Congress said that's not right and passed a bill restricting Congress from Insider Trading, it's so full of holes its called the Swiss cheese bill for Insider Trading, it reads like a comedy routine, if caught, raise your right hand and swear, it was without intent, and let the cash register ring cha-ching!

Congress the privileged few, insider Trading:

Congress was not held accountable for Insider Trading, that information was classified as nonpublic or transparency, simply put Congress had special dispensation from all other Americans for Insider Trading, its called immunity from prosecution The Hypocrisy that Congress has proposed a 28 amendment bill, that would hold Legislators accountable for Insider Trading, It's a preferential myth; when Congress upholds inflammatory immunity to a select few, the Constitution has no such law Congress had never been "exempted" from Insider trading laws, Professor Donna Nagy responded-- Congress has never actually passed a law regarding Insider Trading. What do you call, a one sided debate, on immunity from prosecution without legal representation? Answer Congress without intent!

Insider Trading! Financial meltdown, leaders sell:

It was in mid September 2008, the Dow Jones industrial average was bullish and flexing its financial ragging horns above 10,000. That was before infamy, Treasury Secretary Hank Paulson and Federal Reserve Chairman Ben Bernanke addressed the congressional leaders, the privileged few arrived behind close doors, cell phones where confiscated, the whisper was speculation of a global financial meltdown, Secretary Hank Paulson acknowledged the crucial reality it would occur within a matter of days. Alabama Representative Spencer Bachus, ranking Republican member on the House Financial Services Committee and chairman inhaled as if doomsday was written on the winds of his financial fortune. The following day Representative Spencer Bachus purchased option funds that would increase in value once the market took a one and a half gainer into the crapper. That of course was without intent! Don't get upset with my reference without intent, I only respond to the facts of the magical wand. September 17, 2008, Republican Jim Moran unloads ninety stocks including AT&T, Apple, Conoco and even Goldman Sacks, it was Jim's most active trading day of the year, he did avoided massive losses. Rep. Shelley Capito sold, between $100,000 and $250,000 in Citigroup stock the following day after the briefing. Dick Durbin, the assistant majority leader of the Senate, sold $73,715 in stock funds after the doomsday briefing. On September 18, he sold an additional $42,000 in stock." Dick Durbin's spokesman Max Gleischman ineffectually responded, Dick had no insider information! It was illegal for the American Public to be informed therefore it was just another day. Follow the bouncing-ball of Nancy Pelosi responding, "That she would never act upon an investment of confidential data." Give me a break! That's not conceivable, if you have the god given right, by the position of title, the correct answer, you bet she would and did. Denial is acknowledging it was morally wrong. Mr. Boehner said, "A financial adviser makes decisions on day-to-day trading on their investments." It's amazing, that Congress has a pass, that also include their friends, Guess what! Ever heard the term Plutocratic Cronyism!

Senator Kirsten Gillibrand, quest!

"I haven't been in Washington long, but it doesn't take

long to know exactly what's wrong with it," Senator Kirsten Gillibrand said. "Everyday people are not being heard because too much business is happening behind closed doors. Too often the system only benefits the special interests that have way too much power. My agenda puts the interests of families before all else by making government more transparent and accountable. Senator Kirsten Gillibrand reform agenda ends automatic pay raises for members of Congress, reins in special interest influence on our elections, forbids Senators from anonymously obstructing legislation, and makes the federal funding request process fully transparent so citizens can judge for themselves how politicians are spending their money. Good luck with your quest!

A concept, accountability behind close doors:

Ms. Slaughter and Representative Tim Walz, Democrat of Minnesota, led the charge for the legislation in the House. "The perception is that members of Congress are enriching themselves," Mr. Walz said. "That's not only an affront to our neighbors, that we are not playing by the rules. It is a cancer that can destroy the democracy." That's how you take 60 minuets scathing report on Congressional insider trading, and eliminate the principle of accountability and transparency. Clarification they will not be prosecuted for insider trading, God forbid they are restricted from the Golden Goose of fortune!

A new outlook- 2012 Insider Trading or not:

Senator Kristen Gillibrand D NY and Senator Scott Brown R MA introduces bills S1902- S.1871, the Stock Act a non-historical phenomenon that shows the characteristic constituent of Legislative urgency, 60 Minuets in 2011 aired a scathing report on Congressional insider trading accountability and transparency. 2012, the two main provisions of the Act! Eliminate confidential information with lawmakers and staffers that disclose Capital Hill activities. Simply put, no free passes for insider trading.

The second provision:

It brings forth criminal intent that facilitates investigating corruption by public officials. Sounds like the Sheriff is in town! Now it gets down and stealthy, Republican majority leader, Representative Eric Cantor, denotes the level of complication, therefore he simply struck both provisions S.1871, the Stock Act from the House measure. Mr. Cantor stated that the registration language might constitute problems with the First Amendment issues, a blip in the thought process!

That triggered a scathing dissent:

Republican Senator Charles Grassley, sponsor of the registration mandate, indicated the House retreat would afford professional tipsters, in the shadows, just the way Wall Street likes it." There will be a bill enacted into law; that will essentially have a waiver or a life preserver amendment that will keep Insider Trading for Congress afloat like Twinkies for another hundred years! It's time to make Congress accountable.

House Passes Bill Banning Insider Trading:

Stop the press! The bill goes back to the Senate, Democrats screech their disapproval, saying that House Republican leaders have stripped the essence from the bill, altering provision, the term should have been complete transparency monitoring, firms that collect political intelligence for hedge funds, mutual funds and including other unspecified investors. The Senate bill stipulated, such firms would have to register and report their activities, as lobbyists do. The House detoured the passage of the bill, whether it's legal to require registration of people who collect political intelligence for the use of investors. The Lobbyist with a Plutocratic fraternity of 1% prevailed with Inside Trading. Transparency, "that's not constitutional". Did you really conceive they would kill the Golden Goose!

It's in the dark:

Louise M. Slaughter Dem. NY verbalizes, "it's apparent the House Republican leaders can not endure pressure from the political intelligence community, which is unregulated and unseen and operates in the dark."

Senator Charles E. Grassley Rep. Iowa, who wrote the proposed disclosure requirement for political intelligence firms, Damn well vocally responded, "it's astonishing and extremely disappointing that the House would fulfill Wall Street's wishes by killing this provision!" And the cliffhanger is in full swing! It get's better!

A Twinkie bill:

The House Republican leader Eric Cantor of Virginia, flat out stated the Senate bill was flawed! Representative Nancy Pelosi our California detractor; responded that the bill might just have, "serious shortcomings" indicated the Senate version, "much diminished." Nancy with a commanding posture of a Lobbyist with approximate 300 million for the cause indicated maybe or maybe not! Nancy supported it, with a point of clarification attempting to avoid legislation, I don't want anybody to interpret a strong vote, as a seal of approval." Goody, Goody it should have been called the Mythical Nancy whatever without intent or the Twinkie bill of a hundred years to revaluate!

A Question of Certitude:

Robert Rubin Secretary of Treasure 1995–1999. Robert was chairman of Goldman Sachs before he became Secretary of Treasure. Can the past association influence the future, deception bridges the past impact of one's commitments; only the present holds the truth of one's true ideology. Robert Rubin sparked the controversy of commitment when he attempted to influence a Treasury official to downgrade Enron's corporate debt, a debtor of Citigroup it was refused. Rubin was cleared of any wrongdoing, yet was harshly criticized. The question of certitude is comprised by its own actions. The taste of human flesh once consumed, like the Lioness, it becomes the single prey of addiction.

Citigroup had the capacity of influencing both Houses, on how not to balance the budget. There is a great old song, "exempt the regulations and let the good times flow, for Gramm and Enron it was a family affair." It afforded the Gramm household an excess of a million plus. The bad news Enron went belly up! And America Real Estate was standing in line! Along with a multitude of ex legislators, with title Lobbyist, waiting to deregulate America for profit. A certain Enron Executive bags groceries at HEB, that became his retirement fund, he refers to Gramm with several derogatory placements of where to go!

Milk and Honey! The Flim-Flam man:

The 12th day of November 1999, President William Jefferson Clinton signed; Citigroup Relief Act of Repeal, also known as Gramm-Leach-Bliley Act, the milk and honey Financial Services Modernization Act." It became an international conspiracy, the linguist Phil Gramm dislodged the burial chamber of 1929 prehistoric Black Tuesday, unearthed the barrier of a 16 trillion dollar meltdown, with a duplicitous spade of deregulation a single-mindedness, altered the finical structure, as Wall Street Lobbyist deregulated the financial world, Subprime became the voracious savage beast, a three hundred pound Jackal, salivating and it did pounce!

Somebody asked Phil Gramm:

To explain, if the Seventy Third Congress in their

wisdom understood the necessity of financial reform after the Great Depression in 29, why in God's name would he open the floodgates of fraudulent opportunity for the greed mongers? Phil Gramm smilingly conveyed a mythological deception of the legendary Flim-Flam man with words of wisdom, "it was Congress in a partisan majority vote, that dictated Wall Street had rehabilitated."

It happened behind close doors:

Goldman Sachs self-indulgence set forth a path that ascended into a decade of oblivion. It required Goldman Sachs, Phil Gramm, Robert Rubin Treasury Secretary and special interest Lobbyist group's, it first required Gramm's attached devotion to repeal the Glass Steagall act of 1929. The fifth-amendment provided Wall Street exclusion behind close doors and duplicitous subprime was introduced to the world. It required a massive amount of financial grease and Legislative intent. What happened when Wall Street and Legislators negotiate behind close doors, you have qualified a future prospect for Lobbyist! Can you spell Phil Gramm!

A time to remember:

The siege of depression brought forth the ferret depth of fraud and corruption it was Record March 9, 1933. The Seventy-Third Congress First Session exposed the deception perpetrated through use of Federal Reserve Bank Notes. Sixty-six years later America forgot, yet that memory has never faltered from my impressionable viscera of a generation's desperation, which consumed America without a prayer or God. The Plutocratic 1% that year of desperation traveled to Europe and sent their kids to Harvard.

That Documentary of tragedy, a prose by Mot:

Moviegoer newsreel, 1936 a Grierson's Documentary, into the world of yesterday! The old people talked about the crash of 29 that ravished a complete generation. A rhythmic quarter-tone step trumpeted the sound of the ages, massive lights tempered realism as I sat from afar, an editorial breath projected a pivotal toil of tragedy, once upon when eternity stood still, Grierson's baritone voice radiated "Homeless", a flicker of light amiss, through a tormented sculpture, bore a forsaken destitute for masses appeared, before their eyes silence imprisoned a wandering odyssey, muse was transient for a casteless society, fear inconsolable clutched a spiritual prayer without penance, a calm voice was Grierson tarnished anguish, war veterans, factory workers rode endless rails of sufferance, sorrow without humanity, absence ceased the sunset from afar, migrating farmers, dissolved from a thousand Dust Bowls, across infernal abyss, despair of Shantytowns unsettling awareness, wandering aimlessly on deflated tires, a caravan of junkyard carcass, inherited a misery of desolate haunts, minus a solitary whisper, stacked a grave bits and pieces, an apparition banished the anguished soul, a woman's vacant breath motionless to score, consumed misery unsung furrowed a brow without mark of destination, fraudulent toil condemned a child's despair far beyond oblivion.

A curse all, deregulation:

The modernization act, effectuated the tenacity of Wall Streets acquisitiveness, for bullish trumpeted deregulation, a merger of financial utopia, the speculative yeast escalated a twisted pretzel of unlimited potential, Commercial Banks, Investment Banks, Insurance Companies, and Securities Firms interlocked fingers of unscrupulous profiteering into a mythical pastry of cataclysmic Ponzi bread, the Modernization act became Subprime! A cure all! From the recess of Real Estate financial growth to Wall Streets inspirational saga, an abundance of deception without a tinge of mathematical merit, the Hounds of Lobbyist came forth in canine multitude, for excessive bloodletting, carnivorous was the banner of Wall Street! The Fraudulent Subprime was the linguistic prowess a rendition of Wall Streets bullish; deregulation trumpeted the grand protagonist Citigroup. Treasury Secretary Robert Rubin under President Clinton, insisted that Subprime was America's forthcoming salvation into the financial hereafter. The repeal came forth, Rubin and deputy Lawrence Summers steered the 1933 Glass- Steagall Act, into oblivion, a transformation into the portal of unchallenged deregulation Wall Street became a duplicitous renegade of immeasurable potential with fraudulent intent. S&P and Moody's Investors Services, they stamped the Global seal of triple AAA approval ratings, Second came the heavy hitters, too big to fail fraternity, Citigroup, Goldman Sachs, Bank of America, Lehman

Brothers, Bear Sterns, Merrill Lynch, JP Morgan and Wells Fargo with unlimited resources. Rubin a year later became the Exalted Chairman of the Citigroup Executive Committee, who would have guessed that!

Let the games begin!

Wall Street, Richard Fuld before breakfast was high flying his stock 161 by diner time the bell rang Bankruptcy, without a whimper Lehman Bros was consumed, Joe Gregory COO was conversing at Nobu over a $600 Wagyu beef burger, when Lehman Brothers assets became toxic. The SEC examiners had no earthly conception that Lehman Brothers at the end of each quarter sold Toxic mortgage securities, and after the quarter purchased them back, a complex transaction known as Repo 105 that eliminated the Toxic securities off the balance sheet while regulators and shareholders where examining the books. In case you're wondering, yes its down right Fraud! On the other hand the Federal Reserve bailed out AIG with taxpayer funds, a fraudulent undertaking! Keep that thought in mind, the United States Federal Reserve Would have dispensed 16 trillion dollars without informing Congress or the American public!

Poet Stanley Kunitz final line:

"The bloodied envelope addressed to you is history, that wide and mortal pang."

"So be it!"

CHAPTER TWO

Swayed not so much, Opinionated you bet!

I'm independent past the cynicism of imperfection; I listen to Imus in the morning he's highly opinionated and he's politically constipated to a spontaneous fault, Imus he's a humorous cuss with a streak of honesty and a humanitarian grit, an attitude for the ages. I figured, Imus conceived the value of inspirational at a mature age, he derives with a historical interpretation for insightful review, I scrutinize commentators on a daily basis, MSNBC, Joe in the morning, Joe Scarborough is highly intellectually without a filter, yet you can't fault Joe, he survived the political trenches and placates to Mika's astute judgement, when sanity prevails. Mika Brzezinski a cerebral cortex, with superior appeal for she's awesome, with an air of inspirational acumen and a divine posture of guidance. Jon Stewart genius a political satire of witticism; Jon has a profound facial accuracy that exposes unlimited surgical insanity. Statistically from my prospective Joe and Imus both I consider informative, highly opinionated and insightful from both sides of the spectrum. I find Jon Stewart extends a perceptive of his own ingenious delivery of the wacky political world, where stupid has a PHD and title. I believe everybody slants the interpretation accordingly to his or her personal hypothesis, investigation and "you got to be kidding," a sense of that's the way it was, will interpret the matter of accuracy, the term invested has a different condensation of summary in the political arena, invested is subsidizing greed for an advantage, I'm sorry to say, that 280 million Americans consume a whopping seven percent of the American dream and have no redress for grievances. The Supreme Court deemed the Individual Conglomerate the Alpha of, "We the corporation! Consumed the first amendment." In my day, they would have tar and feathered a few Judges with intent!

Read between the lines:

President W. Bush stated, "We don't believe in planners and deciders making the decisions on behalf of Americans, you got to have people at the top who respond to and are selected by Presidents." Dick Cheney completed that famous line; "you got to have Lobbyist at the top that selects Presidents!" That became the start of a 16 trillion dollar nightmare.

Freddie Mac guarantees $26.3 Billion:

Follow the bouncing ball of the Gramm multi-trillion-dollar subprime meltdown, Fannie Mae encouraged banks with President Clinton's blessing to increase home mortgages with minimal credit and a paltry down payment, this was strictly for conventional loans. Now you would consider that was a generous act, that's if you where retarded or believed the Too Big to Fail Banks where in the business of fairy tales. Real Estate snowballing without thought of decline, interest rates held stead fast, the fraudulent scheme was in the final stage of perfection. Freddie Mac and Fannie May a verse of poetic Subprime, a dramatic reading of Legislative tax free guarantee give away, the Banks Too Big to Fail and the Hedge Fund Suits soared, without guidance or resolve, into a deceitful thespian superlative spin, in the sheltered recess of a fraudulent illusion, a single utterance, Commission! Rang the duplicitous lure of excessive wealth with unlimited possibilities. The Government Insurance possessed indemnity against the burden of loss. The Lobbyist set forth, an inspirational blessing the Holy Grail of volatile assets, they introduced one and all to AIG's signature Government backed Insurance, a Mythical God of Midas lived in a magical world of Freddie Mac and Fannie May. Simply put, Wall Street had insurance to cover their abyss of fraudulent escapades, what was even worse Congress stated it was without intent!

Wall Street Bullish today!

November Fannie Mae buys subprime mortgages $600 million, essentially they where testing the waters of purity and licking their chops, Real-estate value summited into a financial spiral beyond the Golden Fleece, Freddie Mac enthusiastically jumps into the frail of quicksand hype, they purchased mortgages to a measly tune $18.6 billion, the subprime loans have a triple AAA guaranteed rate, except they are the fraudulent apex of the trash heap. That year business soars beyond the grasp of astronomical, Freddie Mac, says what the hell and guarantees another $7.7 billion worth of toxic subprime "triple A" bull rated guaranteed mortgages, "just do it! Yells Lehman, Citigroup, Goldman Sachs and a thousand voices too big to jail rang Commission; Commission the peremptory screech of trillions was in the making. S&P and Moody's Investors Services; bundled up crap and stamped the Global seal of triple AAA approval. Fannie Mae, obediently purchased and perpetrated an additional billion under the Community Reinvestment Act, who cared that they where valued below the death zone, a stroke of insanity ran rabbit into the brier patch of S&P and Moody's Investors Services for they humped the rabbit, for extra millions and upgraded another several hundred billion triple AAA rated seal of goody, goody crap, the Hedge Fund Suits are insured to the hilt to fail. You think that the US Attorney General would classify that as a form of a criminal act with intent. They said fair play, without intent!

President W. Bush trumpets!

Fannie Mae proudly announced 50% of its business will be available for low- and moderate-income families, that's now a half of a trillion dollars in the Community Reinvestment Act related business with a deadline of opportunity that will not expire until 2010. Phil Gramm in 2004 became a Lobbyist with the banking industry. Who would have guessed that! The housing boom spiked 72 percent into the hereafter, and Wall Street was soaring into orbit. A Lobbyist asked, "What if there was no closing cost? Or title fees, or questionable credit!" The Answer was a sweet smell of success on batten breath, "72 percent increase into the hereafter! God Man! Credit check it's no longer a necessity; in fact they don't even need to tell the truth about income, nobody going to check it." Then the Hedge trust conceived an adjustable mortgage, "Flexible Loan Option, Oh my god John just died and went to financial heaven! The option you ask! A secure rate of 4 percent for two years or less, the leverage was to bundle and sell worldwide, it's the investment into the future, S&P and Moody's Investors Services thought about it! And came to the conclusion that Triple AAA crap Subprime Mortgage in two years would orbit into 11% or maybe 12 %, therefore crap is flowing like nuggets of M&M's and fraud enhances the Investors Services for they have become the Global Fleece, they didn't care if somebody defaulted, the property will compensate the loss and increase the value of the securities. Wall Street Conglomerates instructed their Lobbyist, open the floodgates to subprime toxic mortgages, Both Houses, Upper Senate and Lower Congress including the undying participation of the S&P and Moody's fraudulent deception continued, with intent, indulged without a single thought of verification for they heed without intent, therefore not guilty!

S&P and Moody's, the key Trillion $ enablers:

S&P and Moody's unveiled their AAA credit rating, the buzz hit Wall Street's bullish zest into a one and a half gainer straight off the Bullish left nostril, the fray of deception snorted, and proclaimed the seal of S&P and Moody's Golden top-AAA rated subprime mortgage-backed bonds, S&P and Moody's where collecting hundreds of millions with full knowledge they tweaked the boundary of fraud, you say that's hard to believe! Let's do the math, they rated trillion of subprime mortgages, with bad credit and undocumented incomes from 2002 to 2007, and Investors World Wide had the Global seal of Coitus direct from S&P and Moody's. John Paulson had the blue print of corruption direct from Goldman Sachs that AIG was providing Insurance against the Global Crap that Moody's and S&P had blessed with triple AAA rating. The former S&P Managing Director Richard Gugliada stated, "the criteria, was somewhat an inspiring concept to stimulate the economy, by altering the standard rating on Subprime Mortgage back bonds to inspire an increase of corporative profit", that's a benchmark, straight out intent to fraud, the two key ingredients S&P and Moody's upgraded unregulated investment pools of collateralized debt obligations "CDO's" and upgraded mortgage backed securities "MSB" that violated the letter of the law on both counts! That's straight out intent to commit a criminal act of fraud. The Lobbyist, with cash inducement in hand, put their best foot forward and advocated the letter of inspiration was a charitable adventure not, "criminal!" they suggested the term criminal was rather harsh, they preferred misrepresented, altered somewhat, fudged a little, in reality they embellished ratings with a Golden opportunity for the working class folks, it remains a fraudulent act of Anticipatory repudiation, that's a declaration without a shadow of a doubt! That Moody's and S&P committed fraud in pursuit of personal financial gain in the millions. Guess what! The Government Accountability Office beseeched US Securities Regulators to vigorously reduce the potential conflicts for credit rating agencies. The Government said Moody's and S&P had no intent! As a citizen you would be serving 30 years! And your attorney would be committed for demanding a mistrial that it was without intent. And if Martha Stewart is smart she should sue the SOB's, accordingly Martha was without intent!

McGraw-Hill spent 430,000 for S&P free pastures:

The Securities and Exchange Commission! "Was in the thralls of considering!" What you ask? They were mulling over, weather S&P categorically committed a fraudulent crime! It's criminal for Congress to apply the term, considering! When they outright should have charged Moody and Standard & Poor's with criminal intent in gerrymandering mortgage-backed securities directly from the garbage heap into the apex of triple a fraudulent wonderment. The fact, political manipulation interpreted the degree of intent, that's criminal deception, Congress in the 4th quarter in 2009 was undecided by the overwhelming evidence that ran into the billions determining Standard & Poor's fraudulent status. McGraw-Hill, who owns Standard & Poor's spent 430,000 lobbying in their defense of innocent, as the winds of November faltered past the haughty winter of 2011, the memory lingered without a lucid whisper of yesteryears criminal intent, fact the Corporative Lobbyist is afforded the right to deregulate the Constitution for the benefit of a Plutocratic fraternity consisting of the wealthiest 1%. The paper trail of evidence is beyond Congress to resolve with determination that Standard & Poor's was without intent! You be the judge! That 1% fraternity greed mongers bankrupt the Real Estate market, collected on betting against their investors and America, and 280 million Americans suffer, and Congress said it was distorted.

Democracy to survive; must adhere to the principles of

social equality. Yet Congress, Senate and the Supreme Court openly showed no web of intent in upsetting that fraudulent fraternity. The Political and Plutocratic fraternity 1% are fined, for they had no ability to comprehend, try that interpretation when you are arrested, if you believe you won't be going to jail; think again Jail Bird. By the standard of ethics shown by our Judicial System, we have a political Loopy Cuckoo system of corruption!

The illumination from above:

S&P and Moody's found a new religion, the church of every-day hypocrisy, they failed to practice those virtues that they preach. Somehow they received amnesty from any thought it could be classified as incriminating, Congress with a stroke of the Legislative illumination, eliminated any inclination of conspiracy, and Congress proclaimed it was without felonious intent! Behind close doors, a conspiracy became oblivious to the letter of the Constitution, for the economy must prevail! And let the good times flow, it did for Hedge fund John Paulson who acquired one billion on the spot. That beats the hell out of working for a living! I wonder if John ever sold Pizza! Zing!

Guess what, they screamed bonus':

The rating agencies were sharply criticized, your kidding! That's a felonious act of intent, it's a punishable crime, yet the "Too big to go to jail fraternity," received their infamous bonus' thanks to the American Tax payer. Geithner President of the Federal Reserve Bank expressed his attitude regarding the credit agencies. "Look at the quality of judgments they've made in the past." You will just love this bit! The administration had acknowledged S&P committed an error; the fraudulent deficits ran into trillions, I love that bit, look at the quality of judgments, they've made in downgrading America's rating. The fingerprint on the bonus check of each individual, makes a singular statement, it was with a financial passion! And their goes another legislative convert, just call him Lobbyist.

S&P finds Religion and devaluates America:

Wall Street sold fraudulent securities with Moody's and S&P Global triple AAA subprime Golden crap mortgages cost the American taxpayer trillions. The Securities and Exchange Commission in July identified S&P and Moody's as accessories, finding they violated internal procedures and improperly managed the conflicts of interest, providing credit ratings to the banks that paid them. Translation not guilty! Add insult to injury; guess who devaluated the USA for the very first time, S&P. That's what happens when they receive a get out of jail card, without intent, and collect a bonus for passing go! Oh yeah S&P found a religion; it's called the first Church of Congress! I hope the next time Congress tells you increasing the tax, on the Wealthy, is not realistic! Find a new Legislator that believes that fraternity of privileged 1% should pay 90% taxes till the deficit turns into profit.

Housing declines and the Scavengers come forth:

The Real Estate horn of plenty became the burden of

Home Owners unlimited, credit ratings where devaluated and terminated. Wall Street said "oops" and for whom the bells tolled Bullish became the nucleus of Bearish decline, without a thought of survival, as asset went straight into the crapper, mortgages dumped the interest defying barrier, a surge of collapse ravaged homeowner mortgages, the tariff bellowed percentage increase with penalties of "Foreclosure", Global was the criers wares of exotic Islands, COD's faded investors dreams into oblivion. The Greed Mongers where high fiving billions in Insurance the impossible dream, betting against themselves, came into fruition.

Shakespeare's Brutus:

For nobody went to jail! At this juncture what would Shakespeare's Brutus responded, "Into what dangers would you lead me, that you would have me seek into myselffor that which is not in me?"

Lobbyist Cassius at this juncture would respond; "fraudulent underwriting practices, predatory lending, enticing borrowers into unsound adjustable COD's, for I Lobbyist Cassius! Have excelled and you Brutus show no forbearance or appreciation of your ill gotten Insurance, Guarantors of risk with intent of billion!" It was a scam and Congress said it was without intent! You too Brutus!

Hedge Managers, the 2008 global finical crisis:

The Fraudulent Wall Street Trillion dollar deception,

was handpicking the assets that the derivatives would be based upon, then without reservation turned around "shorted" its own securities, in effect they simply bet against the market to fail. That was a criminal act; oops an error in judgement, and nobody goes to jail.

The Dysfunctional fable of Metamorphosis:

Let's introduce the Supreme Court who determined the creation of probability, that an Individual Corporation became an Individual. "We the Corporation." A mythical living individual created by the Supreme Court and time borne the waves of their consequences, "we the Corporation is not a mythical Frankenstein, it's simply a destructive monster! Wall Street's genius was the time-tested flavoring of Billion, harnessed the redress of grievances from "we the people" to the Supreme Court creation, "We the Corporation!

Congress fails to pass Legislation:

"Nancy Pelosi Lied, go figure, she stated without a brow furrow of hesitation, "The President didn't inform Congress! About any Financial Crisis! That I know about." Except the records indicated President Bush Warned Congress 17 Times in before 2008 of the financial turmoil regarding Freddie Mac and Fannie Mae." Nancy I would have had a lapse of cerebral lucidity also. Nancy your special!

September 2008 Freddie Mac and Fannie Mae approached meltdown by 2% of obligation; that required a bailout of billions by the US Treasury in Mortgage obligations. Lehman Brothers, stock registered toxic, they simply filed bankruptcy! The worlds largest Insurer AIG was 80% underwater and guarantee was up to its eyeballs in obligations via Credit default swaps Insurance, we are not talking about a couple of billion, try 70 billion ridding a title wave in the offering by the US Treasury.

B of A acquires Merrill Lynch assets:

In June 2008 Treasury Secretary, Hank Paulson, did not steal $4.5 Trillion, but he introduced the future deficit of trillions! The acquisition of Merrill Lynch with1.949 Trillion of Federal reserve assets made Bank of America the world largest wealth manager and a major player in the banking industry. I have an account with B of A for thirty-five years; they only charge seventeen percent interest on my credit card, because I'm a preferred costumer. It's the same relationship I had with my Mother-in-law.

What's the myth, 16 trillion?

The year 2007 when the Federal Reserve emergency act of 1913 audit trumpeted its findings, that authorized financial assistance, behind close doors trillions exceeded the mark of a 7.7 trillion deficit that was before Congress was aware or approved 700 Billion for TARP Troubled Asset Relief Program, I have embraced Rudyard Kipling poem with the deception of October 3, 2008. Its uncanny the truth was written before Hank Paulson deceptive plea, myth or factual a 16 trillion-dollar Global bailout.

[Rudyard Kipling]

For a moment's breathing space were all one heart and one race panting to shame anew this day of all the days! Treasury Secretary Hank Paulson, Ben Bernanke, Alan Greenspan, and bankers too big to jail vehemently challenged the audit that mislead Congress, for transparency acknowledged the plight of nebulous for the deficit in reality 8.01Trillion globally! On behalf of "We the people, and the Federal reserve dollars!" Myth or fact! And you bid us pawn our honor for bread, we have walked with the Ages dead or last week's wreath decays and you cannot wait till our guests are sped away from with our Past alive and ablaze, the Federal regulators, pledged to authorize 16 trillion, an interest rate of 0.01%, Rudyard Kipling, then you return to your honored place of Faith and Gentle hood of Service and Sacrifice. Korea expressed to Henry Paulson that Russia indicated they could coordinate and flood the market with hundred of billion of Freddie Mac and Fanny Mae, it would require trillions to offset America's ineptness. Apprehension loomed a death rattle for S&P and Moody's Global plague of fraudulent trillions, Residential mortgages plummeted by midyear 2008 into oblivion, the burial chamber exhumed toxic pools of fraudulent deception world wide, the deficit squandered $3.4 trillion without registering Russia on the rector scale.

Myth, 16 trillion or What?

President Bush walked around his desk to gander at Hank's grayish Golden Fleece of deficit, with a good old Texas boy twang said, "Hank, lets keep this simple, we have 16 Trillion in reserve! Try not spending more than 700 Billion if you can help it!" Ben Bernanke summarized the crisis with a tone of burgundy, "the sum of TARP's 700 Billion will not be sufficient for the banks to disperse capital if there is a Global meltdown, it will demand Trillions," Hank simply pulled out his grenade launcher and coerced the Nine too big to fail Banks and the rest was behind close doors the intimidation was from the too big to fail scavengers, they would only accept Billion on a single condition, that there was no condition!

Hank inhaled then exhumed a single word, "fine!" The Banks consumed the assets of the defunked institutions and the cash, and they didn't spill a cent on TARP! Beneath the sun and the breeze it is too early to have them bound, when you make report to our scornful foes, remember we kissed as we betrayed!

Hank Paulson gave advanced notice of bailout information regarding Fannie Mae and Freddie Mac to certain Hedge fund operators; that sounds like insider trading information. Or a reason to purchase Insurance! Twenty-five took his insider information to the billion-dollar bank! Without paying taxes!

Lehman Brothers bankruptcy, say what!

September 15, 2008 Lehman Brothers filed bankruptcy yet Lehman Brothers was holding over 600 billion in assets. The single largest bankruptcy in United States history, and somehow Timothy Geithner and Hank Paulson didn't have an option, that bullish would be castrated on the opening bell.

Wall Street Journal, quoted Lehman Brothers officials stated Neuberger Berman LLC and Lehman Brothers Asset Management will not be subject to the bankruptcy case that excludes its portfolio, In addition, customers of Neuberger Berman are segregated from Lehman Brothers and aren't subject to the claims of Lehman Brothers creditors. It get's better! On October 17, 2008, Lehman Brothers Richard Fuld and several top executives where subpoenaed relating to securities fraud; despite bankruptcy Fuld beforehand increased his income and bonus significantly before the due date of bankruptcy. A fact of inquiry, Lehman Brothers off the record borrowed 18 billion from Timothy Geithner President of the US Federal Reserve months before the final stroke emerged; the deal was consummated furtively behind close doors, what was cooking, Trillions sitting on the edge of disaster! Barclays the British bank benefited from Lehman's estate, an $11.2 billion a windfall for Bob Diamond, president of Barclays from the bankruptcy of Lehman Brothers, yet Timothy Geithner said the assets did not warrant a bailout. Food for thought reform!

No feathers and yet it quacks:

The plausibility, a Republican Tea party Plutocratic Lobbyist orchestrating the succession of financial slavery, they call him Grover Norquist! The maestro was a Bible thumping dispenser of "no new taxes brimstone," to enforce a Pledge of obligation an endowment, for the wealthiest 1%.

There is an old saying, stupid as stupid does, the equivalent, a Republican Congress without intent. If your not taxing the wealthy to start with; then why the pledge takers, they swore their loyalty to a 1% Plutocratic master! The one thing your Pledge did, it made Norquist power hungry and wealthy! As for the Republican Congress' the Pledge, exposed your obligation to the American Voter null and void, for a reality check try the Lobbyist lure on a Jet to untold riches.

An insightful thought:

Former President William Jefferson Clinton expressed an insightful thought, "I should have heeded the concerns, and tighten the reins a little on Freddie and Fannie."

Former President William Jefferson Clinton made the statement in 2008. Food for thought! How do you tighten the rains a little, when you're talking about a 16 trillion avalanche?

Congressman A Davis Democrat had an insightful thought, and stated it with conviction, "I wish my Democratic colleagues would admit when it related to Fannie and Freddie, we were wrong." The Republicans, I believe pointed out that fact!

The handwriting was on the wall in 1999:

Republican John Dingell the Dean of the House of Representatives America's Watchdog stated, the year1999 that the banks would become too big to fail, that it would result in a

Government bailout, he laid out the blueprint for failure, and as usual nobody headed the actuality of 29. John Dingell was quoted, repealing the Glass Steagall act would afford Wall Streets commercial banks, investment banks, Security firms and Insurance companies to deregulate and consolidate. They did! John was right! Words of wisdom from John, "This House is about as poisonous as I've ever seen it in my career, there is little room for moderates. It used to be that when we'd get a bill that we'd really need, we could always count on some across-the-aisle dealings. No more."

Ron Paul said, "I will simply remove five Cabinet departments, Energy, HUD, Commerce, Interior and Education. Abolish the Transportation Security Administration and return responsibility for security to private property owners, abolish corporate subsidies, stop foreign aid, end foreign wars and return spending back to 2006 levels. That's a commitment not an accusation of ineptitude!

That's what you call Presidential! Not exactly what Mitt said on the campaign trail, "I got gold in my heart! You all, I eat grits and just love cash! And my car has a private elevator to the third floor. President Obama signed the table of confinement! "HR 1540 1021-1022 of concealment." President Obama declares he's against indefinite detention for American Citizens. You ever encountered the expression, if you sign it! You will use it! Ask McCarthy."

HUD's negative impact!

The Financial services corporation was created by non other than the United States Congress, their function was to regulate the flow of credit targeted sectors of the economy, and enhance the efficiency and transparency of HUD, they invested $13.6 billion, the following year 2009, the Obama Administration requested a slight increase to an amazing $41.833 billion, lets move forward 2010 a conservative 10.8% increase a gross budget $ 46.344 billion, 2011 a decrease of 5% a gross budget 41.6 billion. The end result was predictable, targeted sectors without accountability, if you consider "HUD's negative impact, was far larger than its multibillion-dollar budget giveaway." The word financial and services within the Government has a deficiency, you don't select an individual that believes nebulous comes after the figure fabulous, try lucid after calculus! At least it rhymes. A great thought by Mot, how many Legislators to screw in a light bulb, one! All others create a deficit!

The Enron loophole Section 2[h]

Phil Gramm, in December 15, 2000, had introduced a 262-page amendment known, as the Commodity Futures Modernization Act; it was part of the appropriations bill that included the Enron loophole Section 2h. Financial wizard Warren Buffett labeled Gramm instruments as, "financial weapons of mass destruction." To date Phil Gramm has faired better than 2h or2g for there has been over ninety revisions or provisions and like the binary system, it takes a nerd with a cerebral 160 IQ to get it over the counter! Sorry Phil you just didn't qualify.

Health, happiness and opportunity:

It's not self-evident, that all men are created equal, for they have become endowed by their Plutocratic Creator without certain unalienable Rights, Health, Happiness or an equal opportunity to acquire an Education, deriving their just powers from the consent of Legislators. The House of Representatives Speaker John Boehner with denial of respect, castigates President Obama, with verbal arrogance, simply defaulted from the embers of civility, into the diversion of elitism bickering, "Grow up!" Please remove your blustering self -importance, Mr. Boehner as Speaker of the House you rank third, respect your title, you have been selected by the majority of your Republican party, ceremonially, as speaker you represents the House of Representatives, you sounded more like a thespian demigod, screeching, "I made clear, at that time, no increase in the debt celling, without significant cuts in spending!" Yet the Health Care Insurance HCAN Lobbyist serves your menu of feast! For nor minced or diced, they gorged on an excess profit of 12 billion, it was accomplished without a whimper; they just removed 2.6 million Americans from private health plans. Affording the elderly to bypass longevity, for the bottom line, legislation for its lack of effectiveness, insuring fewer and eliminating the sick. Congress might not have been in moral session or in reality just don't give a damn, except for their personal bottom line. For every lawmaker in Congress, there are five to six lobbyists pushing their priorities, Health Care alone has in excess of 3,000 registered lobbyists working Capitol Hill, to increase the Medicaid and Medicare deficit. The select joint committee on deficit reduction can't find a Band-

Aid.

Health Budget, $38 billion cut, it's not an allusion:

Health care, the treatment and prevention of illness, that should be the issue, it's the Plutocratic arbitration to live and die by the quarterly profit line. Therefore the policyholder has the noblest of all sacrifice to die. The Republican wisdom; cut $1 billion in grants from community health centers and deduct another $500 million in research from the National Institutes of Health. American's plight to endure another day, it's not Congress compassion for life's psyche Health, fathom a 100 nights without shelter, a child's pain without health care a glimpse to yearn, who crave the opportunity of dignity, but suffer its humiliation and degradation of less than. Health Care for America Now (HCAN) resonates a sense of Mother and apple pie, America's unparalleled grassroots health care advocacy; Executive Director Ethan Rome responded to S.2068, suggested Congress forfeited its responsibility for, "we the people." Calculation; Congress, the total sum of betrayal, billion of dollars in rebate forfeited, Congress the elephantine tusk of protrusion the bottom line profit, starting Health Inc., UnitedHealth Group Inc., Aetna Inc., Humana Inc., WellPoint Inc., and Cigna Corp., a combined profit exceeding beyond the mark of billion. Senator's dismiss the anti-consumer legislation, we have another 2.6 million Americans without Insurance, and guess what! 30 to 1 they are the elderly and the sickest of them all. Do you feel lucky!

The National Institutes of Health cut $260 million:

Medicare theft, has exceeded 98 Billion, my question why does Congress excuse Medicare theft as if it was an error in Judgement? Eliminate Medicare theft and the 38 Billion requested for budget cuts, becomes financially eliminated. A thought of inspiration, don't write a check to thieves without verification, on the back of the check in bold letters inscribe," you will go to jail for hustling the Government! Please remember verification is a point of intellectual legitimacy. The remaining 60 Billion that became Medicare theft is a drop in the bucket. In truth it's a Trillion-dollar rip off and it's growing daily. They advertise on TV how to acquire free medical equipment from Medicare, or! The advertiser will pay for it! Do you understand the term with intent, a cold day in Jail!

Profit before Health Care:

The Health Care Industry Lobbyists, a realistic portrayal, outnumbers Congress 15 to1, former staffers, that where members of the budget-cutting super committee, guess what! They are now called Lobbyist working on Capital Hill. Sen. Max Baucus (D-MT) the chairman of the powerful Senate Finance Committee has 12 of his ex-staffers Lobbying for the Health Care Industry. Congress has become the breeding ground for the future wealthy; they are titled Lobbyist.

Sen. Max Baucus, D-Montana talked about Obamacare, $500 billion dollar Medicare and $185 billion

Medicaid reduction over a ten-year period, suggested Medicare/Medicaid programs will prosper despite the budget cuts, and Porky Pig has a degree in allusion! The Medical Insurance industry simply asked, who's paying? The American, taxpayer of course! By the end of 2012 Obamacare will not exist. Have you heard of filibuster, Congress loves it! First rule of thumb, fire the cronies of incompetence, hire experience and competent, that usually corrects the problem. A juncture of astonishment! Guess who became incensed? Humana, you bet they did! Without a thought of hesitation expressed their dissatisfaction." In a huff of a full-blown tantrum sent the following message to all Senior's, "Budget Cuts would enforce exclusion of unrelated services."

Secretary of Health and Human Services respond, "That's intimidation! Stop it!"

Back in 2003 the pharmaceutical Lobbying Industry; with a billion dollar give away obtained a miraculous multi-billion dollar intervention a godsend with Medicare Part D prescription drug coverage for seniors. Congressman Billy Tauzin, and Senators John Breaux and Don Nickles each held key roles in passing or shaping Part D. All three then left their government jobs and became lobbyists for the pharmaceutical industry.

Ask how to make Health Care affordable?

Eliminate Congress from becoming, "The day of the Lobbyist", they represent the top organizations in the health sector: Pharmaceutical Manufacturers and Researchers of America (PhRMA), America's Health Insurance Plans (AHIP), Amgen, and GE Health Care. The avalanche of Lobbyist are endless, three former Chiefs of Staff, David Castagnetti and Jeff Forbes, Legislative Assistant Scott Olsen and additional staffers with health care portfolios, like Angela Hoffman and Roger Blauwet. The financial DNA runs deep in Political Staffers converting for profit. The Law, Congress or Staffers that hold Political portfolios, must be restricted from Lobbying for three years, classified Insider information, a criminal offense. Close the revolving door, Congress the Legislative body of "we the people" not! We the Conglomerate." Hay! Try the bureaucratic format have them fill out nine forms for review and deny excess trough the revolving doors.

Try following the bouncing ball:

Confusion starts with, a key question, "what part belongs to A, B, C and D?" The answer, the "Plan of desire is affordability!" HMO Plans are typically lower; POS plans are typically higher than HMO's but lower than PPO plans, but all require referrals to specialist, that's when the estimate of higher cost becomes that reality. Next the Prescription Drugs that's the big D part, you actually will be presented with a written estimate that requires additional coverage under big D if you're a terminal Cancer patient, which will include a 20% Co-pay. A painless demise at this juncture would require suicide.

Hospice, can you say alternative:

If your Visa expired then you have Hospice as the alternative, Hospice at any juncture is a godsend, for they focus on humanity for the living and the dying.

The Health Care Reform Bill if passed, Say what?

The first stop will be the Supreme Court, and you can take that billion dollar legislative contribution to the bank! "A five to four vote by the Supreme Court." The Medical Insurance industry regarding Medicare and the financial welfare of the Industry; is absolute! That's a constitutional Lobbyist guarantee.

The reality; in 2010 we could not afford the luxury of being ill, food for thought! Humana first-quarter of 2010 posted a 22 % increase from January 2010 through March, and the Medical Insurance Industry Lobbyist are demanding additional financial assistance from Medicare. Humana total revenue increased 10 % in 2010, to a whooping 9.19 Billion. Then Humana illuminated a profit-making scheme, "Mobile Storm!" They articulated the wonderment of fishing inside the barrel; they suggested transmission of patient's private protected health data to establish a convenient Internet database. It branded the title of convenient, "Mobile Storm Beneficial!" The reality decreases your expectation of acquiring additional insurance protection at a reasonable rate, depending on your health data. Wrap your Visa card around financial affordability, "Mobile Storm Beneficial," its intent separate the financially healthy from the potential terminal. 2012 it worked they removed over a million terminals. Do you realize that congressmen and Senators are being bought?

A what! With a factual discourse:

In 2009, HMHS' Managed Care Support Contract was

awarded to United Military and Veterans Services, a subsidiary of United Health Group.

Now HMHS Lobbyist, and prior staffer from Capital hill protested the Government integrity; HMHS Lobbyist that year spent 3 Million and reversed the contract and who benefited, HMHS' [Humana Military Healthcare Services] won. It's amazing what three million will purchase. The Government had no accountability.

The Federal government is prohibited from negotiating discounts with drug companies. Ask why not! Lobbyist Ex Congressman W. J. "Billy" Tauzin as President and CEO of the Lobbying Pharmaceutical Research and Manufacturers of America (PhRMA) who earns an excess of 2 million a year, that's at least 12 times his congressional salary. He represented the State of Louisiana as a Republican Congressman. Medicare prescription drug bill was a windfall of $200 billion for the US pharmaceuticals industry. That's a turncoat Congressman, and that's just down right wrong!

Fraud, and Abuse a **Training Guide for thieves:**

The Humana Health Insurance provided a training guide, over the Internet. "Abuse and prevention," that illuminated the unscrupulous greed mongers to ingest a course of how to derive in fraudulent abuse. Humana's intent, to overcome the pit falls of billing, except fraud becomes a simplified format. Last year, Medicare was billed for medical services that weren't ordered, evidently somebody didn't verify, all to the access of several billion dollars and adding. Durable medical equipment billed to Medicare that was never ordered or shipped, yet the billing department haply paid without verification. Dispensing services that individuals didn't require or receive, based on their past medical history, you bet! They received their check from Medicare faster than slick on a Goose. Doctor dispensing, drugs, drugs, drugs, medication is on top of the list for breaking the bank. The truth, Medicare system of billing was designed for the blind and deaf; it's like leaving the vault unlocked with a sign that reads, "Samples for the dishonest only." Back to actuality, Medicare is based on trust without verification. Nobody has yet eliminated the fraud or the excessive cost for diagnostic and prescription drugs that's billed to Medicare.   Then came the head lines, how to eliminate healthcare fraud. Socialized medicine, oh Hell yes! That just might work, once you kill the Lobbyist and remove the stigma of "Ism!" I have a suggestion, if you have a flood, first thing shut off the valve. Second fire the incompetent.

President Obama to Eliminate Healthcare Fraud:

Let's follow the bouncing ball back to 2009, first and most important, is the insightful understanding how not to create a solution. The office of Inspector General under their leadership kept a watchful eye on Medicare and Medicaid fraud, the investigation showed improper payments in 2009 totaled $98 billion, with $54 billion stemming from payments made in the wrong amounts, to the wrong person, for the wrong reason. Let's face facts; the office of Inspector General missed the real sophisticated thieves for they crossed the T's and checked the right boxes, in truth the arena of pilferage has been given the golden opportunity to exceed beyond Trillions. It's observing a scoreboard of corruption unfold and escalate into a full blown profiteering of Medicaid and Medicare, and guess what two years latter nobody of importance went to jail and they are still skimming Medicare and Medicaid. The Legislators have thirteen committees that are investigating with an amazing headline of little importance. I have a new term "Fraudism!"

Headlines Nine City Sweep:

Headlines trumpet a 240 million dollar scheme, the largest roundup in American History. "Medicare-Fraud Crackdown Corrals 114 in Nine City Sweep," that's comparing the plague to the sniffles. And guess who's supplying the blueprint, the
AMA Lobbyist morphed the sophisticated Medicare program into an infested open sewer gate for the unscrupulous Physicians, specialty medical care, hospitals and medical equipment outlets. Legislators partisan and non-partisan listen up, the system doesn't work, Stop the scooter parade of you don't have to be handicapped, just a little lazy will do! I's alright for the scooters to block the isles while they shop, except It's hard to digest when that individual picks up his or her scooter and pitches it, with little effort into the back of his or her pickup, with the optional blue flea market handicap special tag, with gun and bike rack. Reset the controls and the rules of the game. We have fifty states and I bet without trying you could corral 114 fraudulent individuals in a four-block area in a singe city.

The Plutocratic lobby Medicare-Medicaid Draft:

When you are toting up the pulse rate of acquisitions that exceed billion in healthcare, hospitals, medical office buildings, independent medical ER outlets and nursing homes the ticker tape of Healthcare Index dividends are on the incline, the Lobbyist are at the revolving door. They have Billion to spend its the AMA draft, Ex Congressmen and Senators are evaluated on their on their Pharmaceutical, Medicaid and Medicare negotiating influence with varying specialty committees, win or lose they will be able to participate as a Legislator or a participating full pledge Lobbyist. Until we eliminate the War Chest of Plutocratic Trillion dollar influence, they own and run the Country, what the hell do you think your vote influences, an allusion of a campaign promise. It's the obligated Legislator who in reality is indebted to a Plutocratic Lobbyist paying millions to redress reform for their master. Your vote in 2012 will only determine which one will become a Senator, Congressman and the loser becomes the Lobbyist winner. Ex Congressman W. J. "Billy" Tauzin became President and CEO of the Lobbying Pharmaceutical Research and Manufacturers of America (PhRMA. A note of interest, 99% of American voters are getting feed up with that 1% fraternity.

Lawmakers and Aid's crafted Medicare Part D:

The MMA established a standard drug Jigsaw puzzle called the Part D plan in 2006, defined in terms of the benefit structure, and not in terms of drugs that are cost effective for survival. In 2010, the standard benefit requires a $310 deductible 25% coinsurance drug costs limited to $2,830. Once the limit is reached, you the beneficiary will pay the full cost, until you're out of pocket cost reaches $4,350.25 that excludes premiums. This coverage gap is commonly called the Donut Hole, the Lobbyist use the term, "synonymous!" as copay and deductible having a fluctuating factor, you don't kill the bottom line, that's profit! That's why we have two and a half million less insured. Within the interim the Insurance Industry will keep on double-talking while their gross profit margin increases!

What makes the pill hard to swallow?

Congressman Tauzin, former chairman of the House Energy and Commerce Committee, who was instrumental in ensuring Part D's passage. Now PhRMA's president earnings 20 times what he earned as a Congressman. Former Sen. John Breaux, D-La., left the Senate to introduce Breaux Lott Leadership Group they received $285,000 from the pharmaceutical industry. They switched direction; they love big Oil a lot better profit.

Former Sen. Don Nickles, R-Oklahoma, helped negotiate Part D, formed the lobbying firm Nickles Group. Bristol Myers-Squibb paid the Nickles Group to reform health care issues related to Medicaid and Medicare, Thomas Scully obtained a waiver, affording to be employed by Alston & Bird Raissa Downs once a top legislative aide in the Department of Health and Human Services, spearhead Part D. a partner at Tarplin, Downs &

Young, now lobbying against changes to Part D.

Guess where Staffer's went!

Wayne Palmer, the former chief of staff to Senator Rick Santorum, a Lobbyist for AstraZeneca Pharmaceuticals LP.

Lobbyist John McManus worked for Eli Lilly; became a House staffer where he was "chief staff architect" of Medicare Part D.

Lobbyist Michelle Easton worked on Part D, converted to vice president of PhRMA, returned to the Senate as a staffer, and once again lobbies for PhRMA. You got it!! The pharmaceutical industry Lobbyist is also at the revolving door of the White House with Band-Aids and grievances, and business as usual in 2012.

A reality check:

Oh yeah, I Believe! That until we eliminate our Legislators from becoming Lobbyist, the first amendment only exist for the privileged, try waltzing through the revolving door as one of "we the people," to inspire a committees attention. It's like a homeless person wanting to be a guest in your garage; it isn't going to happen, he might steal the Congressman's lawnmower. An insightful suggestion for us old folks, try solvent green. A great line for Health Care Reform, a Lobbyist ate the Donut and the Senior Citizen got the Hole.

A Pledge to a Lobbyist!

Lobbyist Grover Norquist a covenant unto himself, a Political vision with tax loopholes for financial compensation, a Pledge for the wealthy. Food for thought, I do solemnly swear that I will support and defend the Constitution of the United States: So help me God. What was your Legislative representative thinking when he signed the Norquist pledge, in reality, said to hell with you and your vote! Let's face reality, Norquist pledge has a bite, break the pledge and the signer has no future, therefore your vote counts for zip!

Norquist Ratio, unequally asymmetrical:

A Norquist refresher course, in Ratio askew; the upper crust top 1% has earned 24% of US income in the twenty first century, In 1979 they received only 9% of US income, that's an increase of 15% US income in twenty-one years. Fair share, a Ratio of Tax rate accordingly, the top 1%, in 1979 was 37.0% of income, today the top 1% with loopholes less than 15%. The wealthiest top 0.01 % percent of Americans income in the twenty first century escalated beyond the fold of lopsided, skewed, one sided, off-center and unequally asymmetrical, and pay less taxes than a school teacher." While the bottom 80 % average income has remained flat lined. And 46.8 million Americans live below the poverty line. And next year gas will exceed the three dollar and fifty cent mark, and Insurance a 12% increase, Pharmaceuticals try cutting your pills in half, Education is on the cutting block for

260 Million Americans, breakfast cereal and co-pay will increase, by then we should have another 50.5 million Americans below the line of affordability. The Government and the Norquist Bathtub, with no new tax, has increased the cost of living; it affects the middle class of Americans, especially those who can't afford Health care, Education or the price of food. Ask GE what's most important! Zero tax or America, I listen to Chairman Immelt on his tax achievement not one red cent for America, I'm sure he's a compassionate sort for the working class! Ask Mr. Immelt if you can sleep in his garage.

"Grass-root Norquist" equals the Weeds:

Grover Norquist President of the ATR is heavily funded by a multitude of Conglomerate heavyweights, Tobacco Phillip Morris contributed $685,000, gambling Choctaw Indians $360,000, Microsoft, Pfizer, AOL Time Warner, Oil Industry, Banking, Insurance, UPS, and the Alcohol industries including Wall Street' Super Nine. Guess What! The Law protects confidentiality, the ATR; they are not required to inform the American public of their contributors, but I thought, you might be inquisitive who's Norquist single largest individual donor to his grass-root cause, Richard Scruggs a Democratic Mississippi trial lawyer, who contributed $4.3 million, trying to limit taxes on a billion dollar fee, Mr. Scruggs provided his opinion when describing Mr. Norquist, "There is an expression, if you need a thief, take him from the gallows." Anybody that signs a Pledge to a Demigod should be ashamed. Billions spent by these confidential Money lords of persuasion, with self- charity in their hearts and not one red cent of obligation, that straight out of once upon a whopper of a scorpion fabrication! This scorpion expressed an opinion, I'm reformed, I have prayed, therefore I might not sting you, but then I might!

A Mythological Pledge, say what!

No new Taxes! Think about Ratio, the majority of Americans pay a higher tax ratio than the wealthiest 1%. We haven't had a Republican vote for an income tax increase for the wealthy since 1990." You got to be kidding Norquist bathtub has oil floating on the wings of Visa. An insightful point of ratio, take 30% from 50,000 that's a 15 thousand deficit leaving 35,000 for a family of four. Take 30% from 400,000 that's a120 thousand deficit leaving 280 thousand for a family of four. The Ratio affords one family the essentials of financial security, health Insurance, Education, food, rent, entertainment and transportation and credit card debt, with a year before they are one of the homeless. The Ratio for the first family accordingly can barely afford, rent, food, with limited transportation, a secondary education, minus health insurance and sixty days before they are one of the homeless. The other 20% consumes 80% and pays less Tax. 260 million Americans have a ratio of socialistic slavery! That plutocratic fraternity1% has no concept, that our grand fathers, fathers and brothers have from time to time given the ultimate sacrifice so we are protected by the Constitution, it say's "We the people!" Not just the privileged. Yet it's fascinating we have exceeded Trillions in bail out; that's just about what the war in Iraq cost the American

Tax payer to date. That's excluding, our young hero's ultimate sacrifice. Iraq 4,756 fallen, wounded 31,938. Afghanistan 2,315 fallen, wounded 10,351. And China is rebuilding Iraq's infrastructure and we like the Roman Empire we are destroying ours. What the hell is wrong, tax the wealthy 90%, if our kids are willing to sacrifice their lives, it's time to impeach about 80% of Congress and shut the revolving door on the Conglomerate Lobbyist. Send Congress and their adult children for a 12- month tour in Afghanistan, the war, will end in seventy-two hours before they arrive.

It's Political Blackmail, and intimidation:

"An undesirable phenomenon." It's a covenant obligation of an infectious disease that demands Republican members of Congress to disregard their Oath, that they will bear true faith and allegiance to the Constitution, and not a tote of substance to an unknown pledge. Never, under any circumstances the Constitution affords any Individual the privilege to sell the American Vote. First and most important "The Pledge," is a direct conflict with the Constitutional Oath of the United States, it's a pledge of single-mindedness to a Plutocratic fraternity, and an exclusive1% of the Wealth has exploited and devoured the American dream! A mind boggler! A single individual by the name of Norquist controls 279 Legislative votes, in both Congress and the Senate Republican House that includes the speaker of the House, the Senate minority leader and all six Republican members of the Joint Committee. The prof of a demigod in the House, your vote is null and void and will never be allowed. There is no compromise or passage, for the pledge is absolute! How in hell did that happen! God knows the term Flip Flop belongs to the Political inflicted.

The Hawk, guess who?

The Hawk is one of the deadliest predators, and cannot be tracked! Grover Norquist [ATR] enforces a Hawk's agenda to consolidate power, benefiting the special-interest Conglomerates, He soars in flight on the wings of billionaires and special interest groups, from a concealed perch he perpetuate the ATR Pledge, not to increase the marginal income tax rate, the problem! It creates a secondary position of enslavement to 80% of American Taxpayers. The voting booth, was our god given right of individualism and conviction, the Pledge affords a single Plutocratic Lobbyist the Legislative control of a demigod. The term marginal, defined as secondary under the Norquist pledge, it's enslaves the bottom 80 % of taxpayers and the unemployed and homeless. 40,000 in New York City are wondering if there is a next meal. Essentially 280 million Americans are several paychecks from living on the streets; foreclosure is a reality thanks to deregulation and Hedge hunters devouring the air we breathe.

"No Republican could expect to win the GOP nod if betraying his party's rank and file, "break the Pledge! You will never be elected again." Guess what! Norquist actually made that statement!

60 Minuets Steve Kroft with a look of dissolution asked of Norquist, "And this was your doing? Norquist paused with a

self-important pompous smirk, in a self- mark of gratification answered, "it's the voters that do..." He paused with a possum smirk of self-admiration, his Demigod ego thumping mouth articulated with an affirmative, "Yeah!" Norquist imperious arrogance was blatantly in full bloom as he continued, "if they break the pledge I encourage them to go into another line of work", like shoplifting or...." and you believe your vote has validity by a Senator's pledge to Norquist!

Spell Demigod, it start with an "N":

Norquist Taxpayer Protection Pledge is the infiltrator of a forged fable, with a Demigods deception, Norquist portrays a sweet Holly Do Goody with a grass root chain saw, the lure of the golden flute, a 1,100 state officeholders, from state representative from governors, Congressmen, Senators and the imposed for they have relinquished the Oath of Office to a blood letting Pledge. Statehouse tax-and-spend interests have observed the inflicted Pledge signers mark, for they appear, an apparition in the dark of mind, rendering the wisp of the ripple, no new taxes, if I remember, Legislators where pledged to represent the American voter not Norquist Wealthy 1%.

Their has never been a law set in stone, except for the Lobbyist Norquist Pledge, of no new taxes, if you betray the Pledge, become branded by the mark of Traitor. No new taxes, except you will pay a dollar more for gas, peanut butter increased 35%; your average medication will choke your pocketbook. Let's face the harsh insanity that Plutocratic 1% can afford thirty five thousand to fuel up his yet and fly to Dubai. 40,000 in New York City including children have no health insurance or a home. The health Insurance industry in 2009 enjoyed the highest profit ever, how did they accomplish that, you ask? By removing over 2.5 million Americans enrolled in private health plans. I bet a billion the first quarter in 2012, they will take a loss; they are going for the long hall in the forth quarter.

Health Care, you got to be kidding, ask an Ex senator slash lobbyist or his key staffers who worked on Committees pertaining to Health Care, guess what! They are now Lobbyist legislating for increase prescription drugs and co-pay. That includes tax breaks favorable to their client, the sad part your vote was bypassed by the revolving door. The Norquist pledge receives billion not to tax the rich! And your going to vote for a pledge signer, I think not, unless you are that 1%.

He expressed his justification!

"I thought the spending cuts should exceed the amount of the debt limit of increase, that makes sense, and there should be no new taxes on the wealthy, the reality it became a Republican Pledge to a self-indulgent demigod by the name of Norquist, The harsh fact, 80% of Americans will inherit the political burden of the deficit. When confronted! The demigod with the Midas touch turned out to be a seventh grade student that expressed his perceptive concept, he said, "I think I will call it a pledge."

"My team is winning!"

Grover Norquist expressed his verbal satisfaction of his team winning, "you ought to talk to Harry Reid! He wanted a 2.5 trillion tax increase last year, and he didn't get it!" A fleeting void as if a sense of self-exaggerated swagger was the mindset of a simple mind glowing, for he truly felt that personal gratification of Harry Reid's tax defeat. The reporter responded with a question, "your team is winning? It's like you came up with this whole idea when you where twelve?"

Norquist, without a sip of hesitation, pride fully acknowledged, "I was twelve and in the seventh grade, when I conceived the pledge."

The Norquist Pledge a sworn rebuff to any form of tax increases, which defined the position of the wealthiest 1%. All six Republicans on that special Committee signed the Norquist pledge. In order to ensure the survival of the richest, it is capitalism that has to be heavily regulated rather than democracy. That might be the reason Mr. Boehner had a lapse of memory! Do you think, just maybe, he was attempting to distance himself from Norquist collusion on a very special day, do you think! It was complicity from a direct quote of a twelve year old. We need to pass a law if a Legislator takes a pledge to an individual Lobbyist they must resign, and fulfill their vocation and become a Lobbyist, after a five year waiting period, for they sure as hell don't represent the interest of the majority of Americans, just the privileged few! That's called a Lobbyist! Past tense it's called a Legislator.

Embarrassed, trying to embrace the unknown:

A reporter asked who's Norquist! Mr. Boehner response, "Norquist!" A silent blemished of distress highlighted a glowing glaze that stretched across his forehead, as if a nightmare arose into the desperate abyss of a shuddering hum, say what! "I don't know any Norquist", several stressful seconds of self revulsion as if a ghostly absence had materialized to betray, again he denied; "I don't know a Norquist", then a revelation of a phantom existence that he was caught between a rock and a hard place, as the name Norquist surfaced with a slight hesitation, "I believe a Mr. Norquist, yes of course, like millions of other Americans, he had shown a definite objection to increase taxes. Yet Mr. Boehner scarcely fathomed signing a pledge of obligation to a Mr. Norquist. He should have asked the Koch brothers, for they know Mr. Norquist.

Paul O'Neill, Bush's former Treasury secretary when asked how in gods name did 13 governors, 1,300 state lawmakers, 40 Republican Senator's, and 236 of the 242 Republicans in the House, sign a pledge to a single individual lobbyist, Paul responded, "simply because they were slaves to an idiot's idea of how the world works." Over two hundred million Americans where not asked or informed of their opinion, take a Pledge, and bypass a ballot for approval, bottom line, guess what! They will not get my vote!

Trillions in debt, and what do you have!

Students with a, thirty-five year indebtedness! And a

decade of Deregulation, and 8.3 % unemployment! "You have the American dream!"

Ratio a Myth into a black hole of insanity:

The ratio of an income, for an Executive CEO in 1960, was 24.5 to 46.5 times the worker. Then the approaching Twenty first century introduced deregulation the   champions of ego tripping; the CEO exceeded the financial capacity into an orbital delusion that greed was far better than humanity, CEO's, income excessed the bounds of sanity, 280, 330, 500 1000 times the average worker, plus the golden parachute and compensation packages. Their within lies a minor problem, its the American consumer that has acquired the financial burden of the conglomerate beast, utopia, Larry Ellison, CEO of Oracle earned twice as much as the cost of the Empire State Building; the year was 1999 and deregulation. That from an astronomical mind rupturing procurement of Ratio, that might be slightly excess somehow, it exceeds a sense of mathematical absurdity, Ray Elliott CEO Boston Scientific total package in 2009 was 33.4 million with stocks and additional options, but you have to take into consideration Boston Scientific did take a loss of 1 billion in 2009. In my era Ray's bonus would have been taxed 90%. An utterance of interest, everything is totally contemptuous, in the world of elitist idiocy, Stephan Schwarzman received 700 million in total compensations that same year, and he should have been taxed 90%. He would have had 70 million after taxes.

Proof is in the Soros pudding:

George Soros the Plutocratic Empire master of allusion. September 16, 1992 Black Wednesday, George Soros broke the Bank of England, he simply used logic, a mathematical fact, it was self-evident, by shorting the British pound, Soros made a billion, ask the British government why they devaluated the Pound sterling. A true Hungarian strategist, politically invested, with a Humanitarian mentality, between 1979 and 2011 Soros gave eight Billion to human rights, public health and Education; it's the Quantum philosophy of balancing the numbers between health, Education and not paying taxes or taking a Nation to its knees. Charity for the wealthy is affordable!

Inside Hedge Street:

Mr. David Tepper eclipsed John Paulson; David wagered that the government would not let the big banks fail or falter. Oh by the way, his Company in 2009 earned 7 Billion buying distress financial stocks, David acquired 4 Billion to add to his personal wealth. Wall Street and the Plutocratic conglomerates will never afford the Government to balance the budget, It's a fact, that 1% plutocratic fraternity is the host to America's demise, they have taken their billion and reside elsewhere, Dubai, Beijing China or they can afford to own a private third Country. David donated 55,000,000 to the David Tepper Graduate School of Industrial Administration; hope they engraved his name in gold. Ps a billion is 1,000 Million that's tax deductible. We need to acquire responsibility, for greed a malevolent virus devouring America into a third class country. CEO Executives vacation, sorry I should have said negotiate in Dubai, tax deductible, in a thirty five thousand dollar a night suite, eating gold shavings sprinkled over their quail eggs, inside an enclosed vacuum. There is an old saying, what goes up, must have a lobbyist attached and it surely will cost the American taxpayer, on the way down! Liberalization regulates and guarantees consumer rights and maximum and minimum prices. That's common sense not Socialism or twenty-seven billion for Oil soaked Shrimp. President Harry S. Truman left the White House with the Constitution in tact; he survived on a pension of limited value. A great American President; who believed in Country first, and God's grace, before fraud!

Thomas Jefferson legacy, Country and Honor!

Experience demands that man is the only animal, which devours his own kind, for I can apply no milder term to the general prey of the rich on the poor. America will never be destroyed from the outside. If we falter and lose our freedoms, it will be because we destroyed ourselves. Don't interfere with anything in the Constitution. That must be maintained, for it is the only safeguard of our liberties. The first amendment belongs to the Conglomerate Lobbyist. Ask the Supreme Court; they have defined a Corporation being a person! A 5 to 4 partisan vote! In Vegas you get better odds.

Judicial review of excess, was the game:

The Supreme Court in its wisdom in 1933 declared public companies must be accountable to judicial review of excess. Simple mathematics if you earn a 50 to 1 ratio your tax rate should be the same as the middle class, if you earn 500 to 1 ratio your tax rate should double to compensate balance and growth. The Midas touch welfare for the wealthy! Congress has a self-serving insider trading mentality! 1929 Déjà Vu, "Me first!"

The world of mythology:

Mitt said! "If I'm President, I will veto any plan from Congress, that cuts entitlement programs, and any bill that raise taxes on the wealthy." That's a financial certainty of obligation to the wealthy. Guess who said it! Try throwing a net over the poor boy Mitt from Harvard. Besides next month he might change his mind. He handed a lady in destitute, right straight from his pocket, a fifty, although he forgot 378,000 he received from speaking engagements, it's a shame you didn't have the 378,000 in your pocket, for it was pocket change!

Class warfare! Who said it!

Irrelevance to a mathematical Campaign Certainty; it's the auspicious umbrella of political Campaign strategy. President Obama asserted with vigor, he would raise taxes on the wealthy! The Lobbyist Norquist said, "He's joking, he's without a prayer!" Speaker Boehner's reaction, to President Obama's asserted position, that he would raise taxes on the Wealthy! Speaker Boehner lit up, tanner than a Hawaiian tourist wide eyed observing lava flow! His verbalization was direct, "It's class warfare!" A pause of insightfulness, exhumed a corpse of parrot criticism, "Mr. President! Pitting a group of Americans, against another, is not leadership! It's class warfare!" Speaker Boehner inhaled to a riff of displeasure; a tearing of lip distress exposed his disdain, "raising taxes on both small businesses and private capital, that amounts to class warfare!" Without hesitation pressed onward, "evidently the President has been listening to his own hype!" A factor to contemplate Speaker Boehner, not once, mentioned his pledge to the wealthy. Stupidity in the political arena has a passage of poetry with a quality of intrigue and it's effective, for it affords nobility to adlib stupidity. "Speaker Boehner expressed that certain quality by stating, "Republicans love stupid Americans. Why else would anyone ever vote for a Republican unless they were dumber than rocks! Yeah, he did!

House Speaker Boehner did that!

Republican House Speaker Boehner spurned the President's calls, for several days. A childish arrogance surpassing defiance without respect for his office, he forgot he was not the President. I personally would have shoved that phone so far up his egotistical self-serving importance of playing President or Moses selling Real Estate in the desert.

House Speaker Boehner indicated deficit sacrifice would require the Commandment of thou cut Medicare, Medicaid and Social Security, but the Commandment thou shall forbid taxing the wealthiest. House Speaker Boehner said, "It will paralyze the economy!" A mythical BC pause of concept his conjecture was precise and direct to the point, "the wealthiest 1%

would cease, discontinue, terminate and deep-six into the sunset of poverty."

Yet in 2012 unemployment vacillates between 8.3% and guess what ever %, Foreign cars, personal Jet's increased sales in excess of 20%, as homes are devaluated bankruptcy increased, luxury Billion Dollar Condo's in Dubai increased, your damn right, its a sellers market, a million dollar day spending spree in Paris without a shopping list, just an impulsive necessity. Poor folks impulsive necessity Wall Mart on Black Friday it's a family affair or a midnight vacation cruse.

The African Slave trade! Poem by Mary Birkett:

A lesson into the human soul oppression, it starts with a single insightful thought! Oppression! Thou, whose hard and cruel chain, Entails on all thy victims woe and pain; Who gives with tyrant force and scorpion whip, The cup of mis'ry to a Negro's lip; Marks with stern frown thy wide, unhallow'd reign, And broods with gloomy wing o'er Afric's injur'd plain! Tell me, ye friends of slav'ry's shameful cause, where shall I find the records - where the laws, Which give to man indubitable powerTo sell his brother, and the spoil devour? And whence do we th'infernal doctrine hold, To sell th'image of our God for gold? Mary Birkett Card 1774-1817

Mary was born in Liverpool, the eldest of thirteen children she wrote a Poem on the African Slave Trade, when she was only seventeen, is a classical allusion of reality. It's about historical Constitutional accuracy that must prevail, or we can all become enslaved to fear.

The "N" word, eliminates historical accuracy:

At Eighty I'm passionate over the verbal and written word and the first amendment, that includes freedom of speech, therefore removing any single word that includes some very distasteful utterance as Kike and Niger from future generations is denouncing your forefathers struggle, the stigma of any given word being obliterated only expunges the existence of its historical accuracy, the thought of penciling out the holocaust or slavery as a distasteful adventure into the illustration of historical accuracy for it lives and dies upon the wings of interpretation. The ancient past that cloaks the temperance of trepidation, degradation and genocide will repeat the finality. For historical facts reach beyond a concept of fact, into a world of mythological acceptance, for heinous brutality wailed the utterance of Niger and Jew not in silence, but in torn flesh and degradation of adversity, if removed, it will no longer echo your forefathers anguish! Only a political conspiracy, that righteousness was its only aspiration. Then it becomes defensible without a shield of remorse. Mark Twain's Huckleberry Finn, they removed the "Niger" and exchanged it for the word slave that's injustice to the truth of barbaric savagery. HR 1540 has a fatality; it erodes freedom for Totalitarianism.

Freedom, that's a thought:

The American vote null and void, like a novel from 1939, Hitler postured with intent, as the world observed in silence, arrogance had an authoritative edge, terrorism was riled to intimidate, deliberate the hand in manor, laced in black, for fear retracted a leathered intent for vulnerability radiated special laws, a nightmare mushroomed intent as propaganda escalated into Genocide.

HR 1540, National Defense Authorization Act:

The One Hundred Twelfth Congress of the United States of America, It's first session, Began on Wednesday, the fifth day of two thousand and eleven. An Act-known as HR 1540 NDAA, National Defense Authorization Act for Fiscal-Year 2012, and the content 557 pages organized by individual every aspect of procedures, naming Naval Vessels, budgets, New Start Treaty, Nuclear forces, Financial Management including reauthorization funding small business. Nothing prohibitive unconstitutional, except President Obama was authorize to imprison an American Citizen without trial, for three years. President Obama firmly stated, "the fact that I support this bill as a whole does not mean I agree with everything in it. In particular, I have signed this bill despite having serious reservations with certain provisions that regulate the detention, interrogation, and prosecution of suspected terrorists." My question with serious reservations, why in hell did you sign it! I know you understand intent!

HR 1540 has a fatality freedom:

HR 1540 Section 1021-1022 National Defense
Authorization Act, Congress authorized $662 billion for anti-
terrorism within the United States and abroad, secrecy intensifies,
arrogance the ultimate $662 billion without specific allocation of
funding, with incipient righteousness trumpets Citizen presumed,
that's the problem, a suspected terrorist regardless if an American
Citizen, just might be labeled terrorist and disappear without trial
or representation, within the darkness of night and detained for
three years without council. The bill is without Limitations, hence
forth, subtitle, extensions, review, clarifications, modification,
repeal, waiver, alternative actions directly and indirectly violates
the rights of American Citizens, by review without representation
be labeled a terrorist and detained indefinitely, without trial or
consul. The table of confinement, inserted within concealment.
President Obama declares never to sanction a Bill of indefinite
detention for a terrorist regardless of Citizenship. The expression,
if you buy it! You will eat it! Yet America in 1950 trumpeted a
gulag's Legislative sickle for thousands of Americans under the
destructive influence of Senator McCarthy, the Senatorial theme,
the US Senate Committee displayed verbal intimidation branding
innocent American Citizens Communist sympathizer in open
session; repetitiously demanding, "Give us names!" Or forfeit your
livelihood, being branded Communist sympathizer.   Just think if
HR 1540 1021-1022 Act in effect in 1950 and Communist was the
menu instead or included Terrorist, America in 1950 would have
dissolved from freedom to the night stalker, a step back into Déjà
vu, when Congress enslaved Citizens labeled Japanese. We must
not succumb politically to a doctorial Government. Totalitarianism,

its objective, political conglomerate supremacy, economic, social, intellectual, and cultural dominance for "we the people, make up 90% of the enslaved."

A note of interest, Michelle First Lady Obama I read an article that you expressed that your husband and our President, was somewhat of a disruptive, mischievous youthful fellow. I figured if you had the insight and tenacity to endure a rowdy, then you should relish a 1831 review from Salisbury, N.C., recalling Andrew Jackson's youth, "Jackson was the most roaring, rollicking, game-cocking, card-playing mischievous fellow, and the head of the rowdies hereabouts." No wonder he started the Democratic Party with a mule." That's what America needs, a Harvard rowdy, with a first Lady named Michelle! Tell hubby we don't need HR 1540 1021-1022. But we sure can use a Michelle for another 4 years.

Politics, Democrat Party, Mot and Harry S. Truman:

I had a mind altering chance encounter with President Truman in 1948, he was waylaid by the lack of funds on the Campaign trail, a Train Conductor, a true hearted Republican, without a thought of deliberation rejected any form of verbal commitment for payment and brought the Truman Santa Fe train to a screeching stand still demanding cash, before that old Santa Fe would choo-choo down the tracks. It became apparent the Democratic Party was not picking up the tab for President Truman's transportation, even those damn fool Democrats where convinced Thomas Dewey was going to win by a landslide. Old

Harry strutted with determination of a Hyena in the hunt of prey; from car to car he expressed his dilemma with a tinge of disdain, Truman acquired the sufficient tariff to transport his single-mindedness to Phoenix Arizona. I was heading for San Diego, I was not yet nineteen, but I sure as hell liked Harry Truman, he physically took after a reporter that made a somewhat uncomplimentary remark about his daughter Margaret's capacity to sing. There I was observing the President of the United States walking briskly towards the baggage area dressed in white including his straw hat, his cane had a life of its own, it had an obedient cadence that stayed a step and a half in front of Old Harry. I was so damn impressed, I couldn't stand silent, so I did the only righteous thing, I yelled across the platform, "Mr. President! I'd sure would like to shake your hand, I'm not old enough to vote, but if I was you sure would have my Independent vote, at least twice."

The President of the United States, Harry S. Truman responded, "I'd be pleased to shake your hand young man." And he did! And he became my number one inspiration. It was the lack of funds that resulted in our encounter, if the Democratic Party had picked up his tab, I would have never crossed his path. He was delayed by the Democratic lack of confidence and I had shaken the hand of destiny. Harry S. Truman performed the upset of the century he defeated Thomas Dewey even the Democratic Party said, "You got to be kidding," the Chicago Tribune on November 3, 1948 headlines read Dewey defeats Truman. Ten years earlier in November 1,1938 a rags-to the impossible dream, a horse by the name of Sea Biscuit challenged the Triple Crown Winner War Admiral, the great son of Man O' War, and the world listened on the radio to a shocking upset by a determined half pint Sea Biscuit. Harry S. Truman woke at midnight to the voice of H.V Kaltenborn reporting a different tune, "Mr. Truman is still ahead but these are returns from a few cities. When the returns come in from the country the result will show Dewey winning overwhelmingly." That day in November of 1948 Harry S Truman became my Sea Biscuit and President for another four years.

I always considered Harry S. Truman and Andrew Jackson had a common denominator their ability to tell it like it was. Captain Harry S. Truman had the distinction in combat to keep a cool head, and never lost a single Soldier under his command in World War 1 combat.

We require an Independent thinker, academia on the other side of the coin, Democratic First Lady Michelle Robinson Obama, academically insightful, a conservative viewpoint, daughter's Malia and Sasha they are the magnificence of a Mothers insightful orientation. I'm 81 and you make me smile!

So be it!

CHAPTER THREE

President Harry S. Truman great quotes:

A politician is a man who understands government. A statesman is a politician who's been dead for 15 years. Whenever a fellow tells me he's bipartisan, I know he's going to vote against me.

"The buck stops here!" Was inscribed on his desk sign, the reverse side facing Truman stated I'm from Missouri. He would turn that that sign around without a thought of hesitation when confronted with a statement of questionable fact, with a presidential verbal tweak of dictate said, "I'm from Missouri, show me!"

President Harry S. Truman determined to end the war in Japan without the loss of an additional million young American Soldiers. Japan believed in death before dishonor and that was not an idle threat. They where incorporating a united merger of self- holocaust before dishonor, General Douglas MacArthur responded, "They will fight to the last individual."

August 6, 1945 Hiroshima, the devastation of a single Atomic bomb shocked the world, General Douglas MacArthur, stated, he did not expect the Japanese would surrender under any circumstance.

On August 9 the second Atomic bomb was dropped, on Nagasaki, President Harry S Truman publically announced, "what ever it takes, I will not alter the course, and those Jap's can be assured I'll drop one every day if that's what it takes." The Japanese surrender on August 15,1945. Even Japan understood the President was from Missouri.

Old Harry was a pistol and a half; I took to him right off the bat. Just for the record, General George Smith Patton Jr. has and will retain his position of my number one ass kicker but Truman is real close. The war ended in Europe and Patton died from complications in a stupid accident. Every body celebrated the wars end, the newsreel showed Time Square and this Sailor was having himself a great time with what I believe was a Nurse. August 15, 1945 Japan surrenders and the baby-boomer generation was about to go into full swing. America was 100% for "We the people!"

The art of being Presidential back when!

Tom C. Clark poker playing buddy nominated by President Harry S Truman to the High Court in 1949. Truman the master at telling it like it was, while being interviewed responded to the question what he thought of Justice Tom C. Clark decision to vote against Truman, "It's not that he's a bad man," Truman paused and then smilingly related without a moment of hesitation. "It's just that Clark is the dumbest son of a bitch I ever met."

When asked about Clark and their friendship, Harry simply turned as he walked away the words floated into the annals of an everlasting quote, "You want a friend in Washington? Get a dog."

Truman when asked his opinion about Nixon without a splinter of hesitation responded; "Richard Nixon is a no good, lying bastard. He can lie out of both sides of his mouth at the same time, and if he ever caught himself telling the truth, he'd lie just to keep his mind from shorting out."

Truman was asked about his view on Government regulations, Harry shifted his head enhanced with that all knowing smirk, as if any forth coming stance of political correctness was conceivable beyond a daydream and a dollar short of sanity responded, "Those Politian's who want the Government to regulate matters of the mind and spirit, are like men who are so damn afraid of being murdered, that they simply commit suicide to avoid assassination."

Five to four that's a partisan Supreme Court:

A plutocratic Lobbying system uses the symbols of government, to regale it self-interest with the seal of legitimacy. Then why in god's name did a partisan Supreme Court of the United States vote in their wisdom allowing the wealthiest 1% to finically adjudicate their own agenda. The wisdom of the Supreme Court confirmed the right of corporations to operate as an entity onto its self, affording finical suppression to dictate political expediency, the rights of the first amendment is no longer valid for individual freedom to redress grievances, it has been stifled by the almighty Lobbyist dollar of influence, the end results dictates financial domination, Senator, Congressman for the victor it's Capital Hill, or your new Big brother Lobbyist is watching you. Only in Congress you can preform stupidity without a degree or a background in Political Science. Hell I call my self a chef, but I burn the cuisine, I can spell it, just can't cook it!

A note of interest:

Ten out of fifty citizens, might name the Chief Justice of the Supreme Court, even less can provide the number of Supreme Court judges. Jon Roberts was confirmed Head Chief Justice an intellectual phenomenon in 2005. If absolute power corrupts absolutely, where does that leave a partisan 5 to 4 Supreme Court

If wisdom equates, then six to three is the number:

Chief Justice Jon Roberts vote was an eye opener that partisan politics rule, making him just another activist judge. A single differential vote by the Supreme Court cannot rule as wisdom or Justice. Partisan refers to fervent of tendency to embrace their cause, not the wisdom; therefore a two-thirds mandates the will of the intellect not the political cause. Stacking the deck is morally illegal; the Plutocratic House of Lobbyist rules the game a hundred percent all of the time. Therefore common sense is to change the rule for balance of Justice, six to three affords a greater intellectual basis of Justice, that's integral calculus. Or an additional vote towards it!

Count the partisan control:

Current Supreme Court judges, contain a magnificent mixture of wisdom and a five to four voting system of injustice, that's partisan control!

Jon Roberts Head Chief Justice Republican! Appointed by: President G. W. Bush in: 2005 age a youthful 50. Said, "I have always supported, and support today, equal rights for women, particularly in the workplace. Great line for a Republican!" Woodrow Wilson a Democrat in 1912 said, "I have always supported, and support today, equal rights for women. My thought was, "when Woodrow Wilson said it, there was no Ruth Bader Ginsburg, and now we have Superior three, I pray for a fourth and maybe if God willing a fifth."

Antonin Scalia, Republican! Appointed by: President Reagan in1986 age of 50. A quote to contemplate, Antonin asked, "Why in the world would you have it interpreted by nine lawyers?" He's a Republican!

My summation, "four would summit a writ, four would be impressed with altering the interpretation and the ninth would be that partisan fox in the hen house, my conclusion Antonin Scalia intellectually knows his partisan opinion."

Anthony Kennedy, Republican! Appointed by:

President Reagan in1988 age of 52. A quote to live by, "At the heart of liberty is the right to define one's own concept of existence, of meaning of the universe, and of the mystery of human life," that sounds Republican!

Clarence Thomas, Republican! Appointed by: President George H. W. Bush in: 1991 age 43 Thomas quote, "My approach recognizes the basic principle of a written Constitution. We "the people" adopted a written Constitution precisely because it has a fixed meaning, a meaning that does not change." A Republican who makes sense, Thomas knows the Constitution and its intent!

Ruth Bader Ginsburg, Democrat! Appointed by: President William Clinton in: 1993 age 60 Ruth's famous quote, "Women will only have true equality when men share with them the responsibility of bringing up the next generation." Democrat! I like Ruth Bader Ginsburg she's the youngster of the ages.

Steven Breyer, Democrat! Appointed by: President William Clinton in: 1994 age 56, A great quote for thought digestion, "I have to, of course, describe the views of those who disagree with my approach." That's a true Democrat!

Samuel Alito, Republican! Appointed by: President George W. Bush in: 2006 age 55 a cerebral breakthrough, "If 'settled' means that it can't be re-examined, that's one thing. If 'settled' means that it is a precedent that is entitled to respect then it is a precedent that is protected." Must be a Republican!

Sonia Sotomayor, Democrat! Appointed by: President Obama in: 2009 age 55, Sotomayor during her confirmation hearing when asked why she wanted the job responded,

"Because I'm good enough, I'm smart enough, and doggone it, people like me!" Sounds Democratic!

Elene Kagan. Democrat! Appointed by: President Obama in: 2010 age 50, being interviewed commented on Judge Richard Posner, "Most case comments are boring because," Elene paused with a slight grin that indicated her appreciation of the Judge, then smilingly continued, "well, because most cases are boring, or, more accurately, because the words judges write to resolve those cases are. But Judge Posner does not know how to write dull opinions." Independent Democrat!

Violence and the first amendment, Insanity:

I object to violence because when it appears to be in the affirmative, the good at best is temporary, the evil it does is permanent, a quote from Mahatma Gandhi.

What if!

The thought if McCarthy had, HR 1540 indefinite confinement; that affirmed a president's powers to confine indefinite any American suspected being a Communist, the Supreme Court in a partisan plurality, would have done nothing, say nothing, for McCarthy would have been authorized by Congress, HR 1540 must be removed, every American, terrorist, Communist or Politian must have due process. It's in the Constitution.

Accused in 52, McCarthyism was the accuser!

1952 the villain McCarthyism, the blacklist was the Congressional game, labeled Communist was amendments deprived, yet Eisenhower shook hands with the devil, accusations became the Tydings Repot! Senator McCarthy verbally attacked General George Marshall, "the General was part of a conspiracy so immense, an infamy so black, as to dwarf any in the history of man." Truman was verbally outraged; called McCarthy a dumb son of a bitch!"

General Marshall was Chief of Staff of the United States Army from 1939 to 1946, was considered along with George Washington as one of the two most outstanding Soldiers that the county ever had. Eisenhower feared losing Wisconsin, kept silent and was photographed shaking hands with McCarthy. General George Marshall forgave Eisenhower, but his wife Katherine Tupper Brown Marshal, did not! She was outspoken to a fault of perfection, "I told George, thank god, it wasn't his hand, or I would have had to amputate it."

Senator Chase Smith, called McCarthy depraved:

I observed Senator Chase Smith with a foreboding uneasiness as she paced back and forth; her sematic manner signified her fierce determination as she shifted her posture to an exacting standstill without a prose of diplomacy inquired, "Mot, what do you know about The Tydings Report!"

"I don't know..." I paused to an insightful conclusion,

without hesitation I imposed a question without inquiring of direction, "are you talking about McCarthyism?"

"Senator McCarthy he's..." Senator Chase lapsed into silence as she opened the folder and turned it in my direction. "Senator McCarthy is a dangerously depraved individual."

I had a single comment, "Yeah, I can see that!"

"McCarthy!" Senator Chase Smith vibrated with great vocal intensity, "That son of a Bitch has charged the CIA, State Department and even the Atomic Weapons Industry of having been infiltrated by the communists, as of now I'm investigating McCarthy's activities, eventually the US Senate will bring Senator McCarthy to his knees; censure is our only option at the present. McCarthy's own drinking problems and his sexual preferences should result in bringing him down by his own perversions."

A prelude to the declaration of Conscience:

Senator Margaret Chase Smith a Colby Collage Graduate, a member of Sigma Kappa with a passionate commitment towards women's rights, in 1940 Margaret replaced her departed husband in a special election affording Margaret Chase Smith to acquire his House seat, Margaret immediately displayed an independent judgment that bypassed the partisan political arena, she voted according to her conviction, the McCarthy surge on domestic communist, she promptly established a major role as an outspoken legislator against McCarthyism, Senator Margaret Chase Smith's Declaration of Conscience, "The American people are sick and tired of being afraid to speak their minds lest they be politically smeared as "Communists," a staunch advocator against Communism a no nonsense Senator, she publically informed President Harry S. Truman that he should nuke the Soviet Union, Nikita Khrushchev in response verbally tagged her, "a woman in disguise, for she was the devil. After twenty years Margaret was considered a Washington insider, she sharpened her spurs with the bleached bones of the miss spoken, McCarthy, a dogmatic Senator who championed blacklisting all domestic communist sympathizers and an advisor to the CIA on Communism. I'm skewed to a fault for not keeping my focus, but when it came to Margaret Chase Smith, she possessed a proficiency of competence that was boundless in the annals against character assassination, bar none. She was outspoken, "it's high time that we remember that the Constitution, as amended, speaks not only of the freedom of speech but also of trial by jury instead of trial by accusation. HR 1540 indefinite confinement eliminated the necessity of trial!

1951 Senator Margaret Chase Smith:

I was attempting at five thirty AM to acquire proper attire for my first encounter with Senator Smith, I was hired by recommendation, not by my insightful intellect, I ventured into a descending zone of less than confident, the closer I got to our meeting I faltered like a mail order bride, I had the right qualifications obedient and subservient, but rejection loomed in the background of my mental resources, as if I was crossed off by the illiterate club of the month, and vacillating the fence with the lack of confidence that loomed from within as a combative aggressor, I inhaled to a silent prayer, being it was my first day, god willing, not my last, it's amazing, competence at 21, conceives a shelf life of self worth within the confines of a cracked egg, I sensed a subservient upright frozen unadulterated stature of fear, as I entered her office, and much to my astonishment, Senator Margaret Chase Smith a true aristocrat, with a strong handshake that accompanied a stare of all knowing. The Senator evaluated every aspect for a point of accuracy, I felt as if I was bare footed and missing my two front teeth, finally she inquired "Mot do you have any identification!"

"Yes, Madam, I'm afraid I do Senator!" All I thought was, God please strike me dead, I was staring straight into the head lights of an eighteen wheeler, minus a single intellectual thought, I recouped to the sound of my own stupidity, "I'm Thomas Mot, I'm on time, if ..."

"Yes, you are." Senator Smith's index finger expressed a decisive indication, up close and personal, simply asked, "Mot! What human does your opinionated mind conceive, will be the next Republican President in 53 and please what ever you do don't tell me Thomas Dewey?"

"Dwight D. Eisenhower!" I responded without exhaling, attempting to regain my composure with a resounding air of Sir; a slight hesitation as I observed my hand extending upward, my index finger raised to an exacting self challenging conclusion, I was verbally venturing into the fray of my irrational opinion, "Senator Dewey will support Eisenhower with an undying fanaticism, Dewey hates Taft with a blinding rage, he sucks up to Truman. Eisenhower understands China and the Soviet Inner circle, the space race alone will eventually bankrupt Russia."

Senator Smith without a lapse of hesitation responded, "Not a chance in hell!" My reaction, mind boggling self evaluation, "why in hell don't I know when to keep my mouth shut," her eyes shifted like a cat stalking my gray matter, articulated, " Ike will be designated the first supreme Commander of NATO."

"NATO Senator is not important! It's consequential," I paused to the realization I had tolled my future insignificance, it became horrifying apparent, the Senator's complete staff entered a resounding silence of my political incorrectness of dismissal; I had just acquired leprosy, for the Senator interrupted with a higher degree of varying possibilities. "Mot, damn you are, a Smart ass!"

All eyes froze like the proverbial ping- pong ball, I observed the Senator's right index finger escalating an upward stance to a slow decline in attitude as if she was determining to drop a few additional syllables onto my insightful stupidity, she exposed a slight grin and retorted.

"I'll be! You might be right, Eisenhower is a possibility, Mr. Mot."

Behind close doors, Her commanding vernacular was determined and precise, she informed a certain Senator, that will remain nameless, "any half witted damn fool would understand McCarthy's intent," then without flinching she verbally retorted, "Senator you should fetch yourself a half wit." On another special occasion the President requested the Senator's presence pertaining to a particular bill, President Truman remarked it was essential for the economy, her reply, "Mr. President you have a perfectly wonderful attitude about you bill, but I don't." The State Department and even the White House, was sufficiently aware that Senator Chase Smith was going to make them earn every stitch of her provincial determination.

The first week I encountered Roy M Cohn:

Roy M Cohn was infamous at twenty-three, not for the Julius and Ethel Rosenberg trial, he convinced Judge Irving Kaufman to impose the death penalty for both, it was beyond delusional, America would not electrocute a mother, yet both where electrocuted. She never received a fair trial.

I observed McCarthy on that momentous day, as McCarthy ventured into a head count of Communist from the artifacts of his Illuminating imagination, directly to a Senate Committee. I noted Roy M Cohn sitting next to McCarthy conversing, he altered his body in a forward position, both hands interlocked, as if prayer just primed the idiot McCarthy to perform, McCarthy shifted his eyes directly at Roy Cohn as he adjusted the microphone, a thespian rendering of self-importance, a sense of intensity held court, a drawn silence awaited infamy for that magical number, suddenly his voice crackled to a drawn silence, "I have … in my hand," a lingering split second, held hostage, "two hundred and five Communist, that the Secretary of State is well aware of their status, they are shaping the policy of our State Department." The Senator's by the sheer lack of soundness, sat speechless to a rendering without authenticity, as wonderment bypassed cynicism. 205 buttonholed an impressive slice of skepticism; the sheer number was the inspirational maestro of Roy M. Cohn accumulative influx, the puppet wizard swelled with pride, a strange murmuring as McCarthy with a dead stare of intensity, pounded his finger directly at the yellow pad, all eyes quickly shifted back towards Cohn for conformation, then McCarthy directly faced the committee and proclaimed, "I have just been informed, the CIA has thirty three known communist sympathizers."

The Republican Congress eclipsed the yellow caution light, McCarthy's scrutinizing web of questionable loyalty; by 1952 he excelled self-esteem into the righteousness of stupidity. "It now has become, the great crime of the Truman administration, President Truman is not master! In his own house, we are not free of Communism! They belong to a larger conspiracy, directly from Moscow.

" My God! That stupid bastard! I thought," McCarthy your out of your mind, I had the good fortune to be at that infamous press conference when President Harry S Truman answered McCarthy's accusation. The infamous News Conference Key West a reporter asked Harry S. Truman, "Mr. President, do you think Senator McCarthy is getting anywhere in his attempt to win the case against the State Department?"

The President shifted his eyes, with a look of disdain as if the reporter had lost his mind along with his good sense, retorted with an incisive point of clarification, "What case?" The Reporter inhaled to an insightful pause, a single thought was projected in his verbal facial mannerism; that by the grace of god he might have been blessed with the scoop of a lifetime, he Inhaled to a verbal inquire with a striated staunchness of persistence asked. "Do you think Sir, that Senator McCarthy can show any disloyalty exists in the State Department and your Administration?"

The President without a sniped of scissor hesitation expressed his assessment, "I think the greatest asset that the Kremlin has, is Senator McCarthy!"

The Reporter reeled forth absent of hesitation, as if destiny had bequeathed a newsworthy intervention of certifiable possibilities asked, "Would you care to elaborate on that?"

The President shifted his eyes to a sharp trait of irritation, responded bluntly, "Son I don't think it needs any elaboration," paused to articulate his claim of intent, and said, "I don't think it needs any additional elaboration."

Senator Margaret Chase Smith said it best:

It is strange that we can verbally attack anyone else without restraint and with full protection and yet we hold ourselves above the same type of criticism here on the Senate floor. Surely the United States Senate is big enough to take self-criticism and self-appraisal. Surely we should be able to take the same kind of character attacks that we "dish out" to outsiders. It never happened.

Welch asked, McCarthy came tumbling down:

McCarthy's downfall came in 1954 when he charged the U.S. Army with being "soft" on communism. The Army responded with charges against McCarthy, the anointed McCarthy believed he had reached the status of God and imploded during the nationally televised Army-McCarthy Hearings, America observed McCarthy in full pursuit of his insanity without foundation as he plummeted into the abyss, when Attorney Joseph Welch representing the U.S. Army gave him a lethal verbal-lashing, Welch simply inquired of the Senator whether he had any sense of "decency." America had enough and in December of 1954 the U.S. Senate censured him. McCarthy died in 1957, still holding office as a United State Senator, and a shot glass.

One of a kind:

Roy M Cohn was an impenetrable figure, he was lethal against homosexual rights, and he was a homosexual, he was Jewish, and mockingly used anti-Semitic putdowns. He died of Aids owing the IRS reportedly $9 million. On August 6, 1986, Cohn was disbarred for ethical abuses, forgery, stealing and attempting to defraud a client. He died several days later, and with his last breath was going to take legal action against the IRS.

Kidnapping is beyond harassment:

The President swears never to enforce the HR 1540 Bill or dispute such a possibility of harassment; False imprisonment of an American Citizen is beyond harassment it's kidnapping the Americans 5th Amendment. Congress affirmed the authority of the President to detain any individual suspected of terrorism regardless of Citizenship under the law of war; don't kid yourself, the Authorization exist [Public law 107–40; 50 U.S.C. 1541] McCarthyism started with appropriate pursuant of a single accusation, in the 1950's, it mushroomed into a nightmare!

Germany started with propaganda that escalated into annihilation of 11 million humans, classified Genocide.

19th President, Rutherford B. Hayes 1877:

"It is now true that this is God's Country, if equal rights—a fair start and an equal chance in the race of life are everywhere secured to all. And nothing brings out the lower traits of human nature, like office seeking." And a Lobbyist with an agenda!

President Obama's sleepwalking:

I personally admire Obama, he's a class act, but he wasn't trained as a Plutocratic beast killer for he was sleepwalking when he received his campaign promises from the Legislative ghosts, headlines to be deceived by, President Obama's presidential order restricting the role of lobbyists! That's like telling a cannibalistic spirit to consume plankton; the Lobbyist has become a scathing savage of financial domination, dictating its agenda behind close door with an iron fist of supremacy. The headhunters, prediction for 2013 the Conglomerate Lobbyist draft, Ex-Republican Senator and Congressional Senior Staffers on special committees, are the first round picks for the annual million-dollar club. The biggest offers are direct from Banking and lobbying firms. There are approximate 6,700 former congressional staffers and lawmakers with tremendous clout with unlimited excess through the revolving door, Wall Street Lobbyist will spent billion with intent to influence. The Mythological legend of the Ex

Congress lobbyist, with a mythological twist, a Senator becomes empowered by the people, as his heart and congressional seat evaporates, that's when the string of influence comes into play, known as the Legislative turncoat wonderment, an Ex- Senator Lobbyist tied to a bill of Arbitration, it's the gateway to perdition tied to a Senator's financial obligation, end results deregulation to enhance a Conglomerates end results the bottom line, profit. Oh I forgot on the other end of that string, is that Ex Senator's taxpayer-funded pension, I don't have charity for a wealthy turncoat making millions on the back of the American voter.

Forbid! Not conclusive, a Campaign promises:

Why beat an inspiring young stallion to death, with a campaign promise, "Shakespeare" said, tell me where is fancy bred, or in the heart or in the head? How begot, how nourished? Reply, reply, It is engender'd in the eyes, with gazing fed, and fancy dies, in the cradle, where it lies, its a superlative piece of skillful manipulation! "Not using the word Forbid!" The word forbid has a spectrum that's truly defined in definition, ban, prohibit, outlaw, rule out, exclude and even putting the kibosh on. To a Harvard Politician that's a Shakespearean career move; oh wonder not! The prof, Obama became President, he did pay attention in class to Shakespeare, I'll let you be the judge, the Campaign promise was of inspiration, "Former lobbyists would not be allowed to work on regulations or contracts related to their past employer for two years!" That's telling a three year old, "don't!"

Obama signed that executive order like Flash Gordon at the pearly gates on a skateboard with a Cadillac tailfin, except it had a loophole that eliminated the thought Forbid! It was called a "waiver" that's when "don't would have been without intent." The administration collectively in their wisdom conceded and allowed former lobbyists to propagate great wealth, therefore partisan compromise, was the essence of the ruling elite, simply compromised a Campaign obligation, and introduced a waiver for the Lobbyist to serve. And fancy dies, in the cradle, where it lies. A great one liner, for your second term! The waver is mightier than the pen.

The Bill of Lobbyist and the First Amendment:

The first Amendment to the Constitution, Freedom of Speech, Press, Religion and Petition The first amendment inscribed the right of the people peaceably to assemble, and to petition. Its Inscribed, the right of the people! In the context, all legislative Powers herein shall be vested in a Congress of the United States, which shall consist of a Senate and House of Representatives. Yet the Supreme Court did encroach with Justice that an Individual Corporation has the right to rewrite and redress their personal grievances on Capital hill.

Universally accepted definition, 'say what'!

Equality and freedom, the question that really bothers me, our Forefathers wrote down in stone that every Vote had equal weight, and they died for that right, yet somehow in the twenty-fist century our Vote has been decimated from a true heroic value, the Conglomerate jugglers came forth with arbitration, and gave birth to a 7 Trillion-dollar giveaway, without obligation to the American voter, it became a pledge of obligation to the Wealthy 1%, no new taxes! Ask Norquist or Wall Street about Ratio of excess.

Congressional appeasement:

1933 Glass-Steagall act created financial stability for 65 years, a lament in verse without a vision of prosperity, the Plutocratic fraternity deregulated and visualized a self serving concept of financial wealth, a deceitful fable, a pledge that lies in the Ratio of excess.

1933 documented the American Tobacco Company President George W. Hill procured a $1.3 million dollar salary, a mark of irritation the shareholders expressed lynching; after reflection they filed a lawsuit, George W. Hill's Ratio of earnings didn't equate to financial stability. The Supreme Court equated that public held companies must be accountable to judicial review of excess. "A company has limited growth if its compensation is not proportionally distributed." It's still on the books!

In Excess!

A suite in Dubai accommodations thirty five thousand per night, a self-serving lure of elitism, for those who can afford excess, it's tax deductible and more important their Xe Service personal are also tax deductible. And the Suits on Wall Street brag openly regarding $600 tax-deductible lunches, private rental jets, all to the tune of tax deductible. And our Educational system and Educators must suffer the pangs of limited resources and reduction in income, when did America become enslaved to the elite1% that preach excessive wealth was their American heritage. When children have no hospital care, a roof to sleep under, and go to bed hungry, our heritage is exploitation of millions of Americans, Tax the wealthy 90% until the deficit equates zero! Eisenhower did and we prospered.

Ratio of Balance GE's appeasement of compensation excelled beyond Tax infamy, the affluent 1% accentuated the fulfillment of capitalism". GE $14.2 billion Globally and $5.1 billion from within the United States, and procured a tax benefit of $3.2 billion in welfare. Cause and Effect! Jeff Immelt bragged of his plethora of tax lawyers an inspirational achievement, echoed forth the ecstasy of legally paying zero taxes!" General Electric closed 30 plants and terminated 19,000 workers by 2008; Jeffrey income an excess of $22 million last year. GE and Iran have been doing business as usual. They published a statement all contracts ended in 2008, yet in 2012 they are still in contract, ask China.

John Samuels, GE's cerebral tax genius, had a mystical slogan, "Imagination at Work!" or, "goody, goody only fools pay taxes!" Samuels' ingenuity, go directly to the source the Internal Revenue Service employees, then include the majority of tax-writing committee ex-executives direct from Congress.

President Obama named Jeffery Immelt GE's executive officer to replace Federal Reserve Chairman Paul Volcker. That's like replacing the Pope, for a Pedigree Pit bull with a personal agenda. Cause and Effect! Affording the top 1% to redress billion in subsidies, and we the people, acquired trillions in deficits. The Day of The Lobbyist became a Wall Street inspiration that was enhanced by a Pledge. Written by a twelve year old!

The Paul Volcker rule:

Paul Volcker was Chairman of the Federal Reserve from August 1979 to August 1987 he served under President Jimmy Carter and President Ronald Reagan, his credentials rise above criticism, he initiated the harsh realities into focus, inflation! The Volcker rule, understand the problem not the blame, he intellectually changed the rules and ended the high levels of inflation.

In 2009 as Chairman of the Economic Recovery Board Paul Volcker called for new rules to curb ill-advised risk-taking by banks, and eliminate the fraudulent speculation that created the financial crisis. Paul Volcker outlined his proposal for regulation in a three-page letter to President Barack Obama. It required two years before the proposed regulations known as the Volcker Rule finally emerged. Wall Street Law firm Sullivan & Cromwell slash Lobbyist, with Senior Staffers direct from the revolving door, actually wrote the final summary of the Volker Rule, guess what! The Volcker text exacerbated the Volker Rule to 298 pages; accompanied by 1,700 questions and topics. It's a crime when Wall Street firms spend millions to modify the Volcker rule, the analysis of Reckless Risk, simply tweaked the concept. The Senate voted against the Volcker rule. The Lobbyist key ingredient, they turned it into a Potboiler! It's the artistry of squandering America for a Plutocratic fraternity of power. Obama named Jeffery Immelt GE's executive officer to replace Volker as Federal Reserve Chairman. And you want to stop the bleeding! Not if you're in bed with a Vampire.

A wisp of protest:

The day of protesters, they appeared like the avenging horde of nomads, they where the homeless, Veterans who came home to endure foreclosure, they besieged New York's financial distract in defiance to Wall Streets dictatorial absolutist 1%. Headlines challenged the legitimacy of homeless, so it was written like the disobedient nomads of mythology, they where devoured by a magic place called less than!

Hire a Crony and Nobel Prize Idiot:

President Obama's administration gave Solyndra LLC, $527 million dollar loan guarantee; it was a great plan, except a small indiscretion of judgement. Energy Secretary DR. Steven Chu received a Nobel Prize in physics, yet was neglectful, in the properties of responsibility, he didn't investigate Soly-drama integrity, the Energy Department hires a former sports fitness executive Steve Spinner, to supervise Solyndra loan guarantee program. Wife Allison Spinner's a partner at Wilson Sonsini Goodrich & Rosati, received $2.4 million in federal funds for legal fees involving the loan guarantee to Solyndra. John Spinner was actively involved in the panic game! August 28, 2009 Spinner's E-mail, How -- hard is this? What is he waiting for? The DOE official was put on notice, urgency was the criteria, second Spinner E-mail, I have the OVP Office of the Vice President and WH the

White House breathing down my neck on this matter. They are getting itchy to get involved. From the E-mail Spinner had full knowledge that Soly-drama was in default with its manufacturing facility, violated the agreement with the Department of Energy. Soly-drama filled bankruptcy, the harsh reality of humiliation 1,100 employees where terminated. Next you need to ask! Was President Obama embarrassed, Yeah! Conflict of interest, No! If you must ask! Try Cronyism that might be a point of consideration!

I have a suggestion for the Department of Energy; try a large-scale systematic plan of immediate termination, if you don't know why! Then you got to be kidding! It's called incompetence, in the first order of cronyism!

The Great Campaign one liner:

"Norquist deceptive Political game," that's double-talk, for bypassing actuality for the magic wand subsidies and loopholes, the lack of Social responsibility diverting from Mathematical absurdity, into a mythological financial chopping block. Medicare, Medicaid, Education and Social Security are number one on both the Republican and Democratic 60 billion-dollar deficit reduction hit parade. The Norquist pledge, get elected with a great one liner, "No new taxes! As for the poor, it should be called the poor mans burden!" In 1999 deregulation became the orbit deficit, Wall Street traders, have acquired billions without taxing them their fair share 90%, John Paulson's Carried Interest, has afforded him the back burner, not a single red cent taxed on his Billion. Your Legislators determined Schools and Teachers should be sanctioned as part have the deficit reduction, and the same yardstick for Police and Firemen no back burner beyond the soup line. If you're the wealthiest 1% on subsidies welfare, The trick: "it's called, Carried Interest, Paulson's billions, remain in the hedge fund, therefore his taxes are deferred, John Paulson, and an additional 25 billionaire investors including GE, pay nothing." They are on the hunt for the next tax free billions; somehow Congress is most concern about their financial future, the wealth of laurel, intertwines the Lobbyist and Congress into a financial association of mutual benefit. That's with intent, yet Congress dictates at their indiscretion without criminal intent, by outside influence, that's also criminal intent!

Abacus 2007-AC1:

The SEC's case against Goldman Sachs' "Abacus 2007-AC1", Paulson & Co paid Goldman Sachs $15 million to create and market Abacus. Fabrice Tourre a Goldman Sachs Executive played a significant role in affording Paulson to choose the subprime mortgage-backed securities that would be downgraded within a short period of time, and the rest is history, Paulson purchased Insurance on the basis that the subprime mortgages where crap and would decline.

The Genius had abacus 9 Billion and Zero taxes:

John Paulson was not a skeptic but a realist, Goldman Sachs flat out predicted the subprime mortgage market was crap on quick sand, and John Paulson did what his instincts demanded, he bet against Phil Gramm's subprime give away, which earned John approximately a billion for starters, sounds like Insider Trading, following the logic that subprime securities was triple A crap, and on that basis John Dillinger was as an undercover agent for Wall Street. John purchased credit protection on subprime mortgages. The "AAA rating" that Moody's Investors Services and Standard& Poor's rating Service put their seal of approval on. They hustled deceit into a fraudster of full intent, that was orbiting on the fast track into millions daily, the Hedge fund crier with toxic grandeur was hawkish beyond infinity. Before the financial crisis hit, John Paulson, invested $22 million in a credit default swap that eventually paid off, it gets better, the federal government opted not to rescue Lehman Brothers. That gave John a staggering insight into the 4 billion give away, and the Taxpayers indirectly was handed the bill. And you conceive that your vote counts, you pull a lever while the Lobbyist spends billion for legislative influence that's Insurance against the American Voter. I have a question should Hank Paulson have rescued Lehman Brothers and saved 3.5 billion, why did they force Lehman Brothers into chapter 11bankruptcy? A luminary VIP from Harvard inappropriately misplaced the calculator. Did you ever give thought you might be burning the Constitution!

Why pay taxes!

The top 25 Hedge Fund managers collectively earned in excess of $25 billion last year, and they have their own Carried Interest tax rules. That rules does not apply to Educators, Firemen, Police officers, or the active combat Military.

Love 2% interest:

Question what if John Paulson needs capital? That's simple he borrows against his Carried Interest, Why! Its called low interest rate its in the scope of 2 %. A Head Hunter or Manager should be classified by the IRS as an individual and should be allowed four thousand carried interests, don't you think? You think John Paulson went riding into the sunset, not in this lifetime, just be patient; he's not gone by a long shot! John is Legislating for Tax dollars, asks John Paulson, and his two associates about One-West Bank Group LLC.

Your Tax dollars, One West and FDIC:

FDIC the Federal Deposit Insurance Corporation, acquired Indy Mac a Federal Savings Bank, and in March 2009 appearing on the horizon One-West Bank Group LLC, a newly-formed thrift holding company owned by several Wall Street international players, Goldman Sachs Vice President Steven Munchin, world renowned Goldman Sachs billionaire investors George Soros and Hedge Fund king John Paulson. They acquired by acquisition the Banking operations of IndyMac Federal Bank from FDIC, and then One-West Bank Group structured a newly formed bank, "One-West" with 33 branches in California, total assets purchased an approximate 16 billion. One-West now operates the national mortgage banking business that was acquired from IndyMac they modify mortgages in accordance with a program created by the FDIC. Let the games begin, short sale cash offer! Pass foreclosure and collect tax dollars. It's like asking a Politician, what is redress? No matter what the Politician says, the hypothesis in the Political world, redress equates Wall Street Lobbyist's interaction for deregulation.

Phase-Two, Tax dollars and FDIC at work

One-West for argument sake has acquired a foreclosure mortgage of $478,000 plus he attaches an additional $7,200 for six missed payments known as garbage fee, a new total of $485,000. The loan purchased by One West from FDIC was 70 cents on the dollar, total cost to One-West $334,600.

Now follow the bouncing ball, it's important to remember the term short sale cash offer, lets take the original $485,200 "that's what was originally owed on that foreclosure mortgage," now you simply deduct on paper $241, 000 that's what One-West is going to pay, now it gets interesting, One-West will declare they have acquired a loss of $ 244,200. They simply deducted what they agreed to pay, that's the $241,000 from the original $485, 200. Now this is where your tax dollars get involved! The FDIC wrote One-West a check for 80% of their loss, FDIC handed One-West a check for $195,360 and your tax dollars also paid the $241,000, yeah! Take your time and just add it up! One-West has received a check from FDIC total of $436,360, and remember what? One-West purchased that $485,000 loan for 70 cents on the dollar, $334,600! FDIC with the stroke of the almighty pen, One-West made a profit of $101,760. Now One-West goes in for the stomach crunching free for all greed blood letting, the FDIC sold the house for 70 cents on the dollar, 30% less than the full amount of $485,000 loan. One-West legally obligates the original borrower who when belly up into foreclosure to pay the $75,000 difference. FDIC requested additional funds from the Treasury. Hell we should get Goldman Sacks Lobbyist to sign those checks; they made it possible. Hell the Mafia asked; could you really do that? Push a key on the computer, and make a million or two.

The Tax Liquidity Ratio relation:

Lets starts with 2012 current collected Tax assets, and the Governments current spending liabilities and a balance sheet of Trillion in the red column, last month. These ratios are important in measuring the ability of our Government to meet both its short-term and long-term obligations. The formula Current Ratio equals Total Current Assets, which we have none, plus the Total Current Liabilities, which we have to the tune of trillions and climbing on a daily basis. Only in the Political invested world of corruption can a fraternity of 1% dictate paying zero taxes and conceive balancing the budget on the backs of the middle class a reality.

2012 became the world of mythological wonderment, no new Taxes, you got to be kidding! Once upon a Norquist Pledge, in a far away place called Capital hill a economic stimulus package of 787 billion was approved by Congress, 16 trillion was on the side lines, guess who was going to receive the trillions, the wealthiest 1%. They ripped of trillions with fraudulent subprime mortgages with the blessing of Wall Street and Capital Hill; they bundled up the Golden crap and sold investors fraudulent triple AAA ratings. And the American Real Estate declined without a shutter of light, and our unemployed excelled the mark of 10%.

Jack Abramoff was quoted, "I was actually thinking of writing a book, the idiot's guide to buying a Congressman, you do realize, that most Congressmen don't feel they're being bought. Most Congressmen, I think, can in their own mind justify the system." I was intrigued at Abramoff's total detached honesty.

Evolution and Globalization:

The 'expenditures of Globalization, known as the 10 giant loopholes cost the government $125.6 billion last year, that's what came into the daylight.

Globalization, Conglomerate Lobbyist deregulation mind set have adopted a compelling off shore mentality, cheap labor, eliminate paying taxes. And according to GE they have circumvented the oppressive tax regime by crossing national borders lock stock and X ray barrel into a Tax free, China.

Pfizer a Globalization cycle of seven years has dispensed with over 59,000 jobs, while Pfizer including additional Pharmaceutical companies are basically once again coercing Congress to declare a tax holiday with an arm-twisting influence of substantial leverage of persuasion, it's Pfizer's off shore profits that are parked overseas. Seven years ago Congress declared a tax holiday, to celebrate. Pfizer tax burden declined from 35 percent to 5 percent, the Government gave immunity to $85 billion from federal taxes, and Pfizer repatriated over $300 billion in profits. And Congress; did not conceive the globalization light bulb was flickering. You want Pfizer and about several thousand other Corporations to hire American Employees, introduce in 2012 a Global Conglomerate bilateral Tax covenant, eliminate double taxation, promote the FDI through an effective tax rate, the incentive jobs. Tax incentive procures taxable profit and jobs. You eliminate immunity every seven years and the loss Globally becomes the mark of Trillions.

Try fixing the problem:

Globalization has become the Twenty First Century supplemented labor force a clandestine enterprise of Tax loopholes and billion undeclared profit. It's the evolution of revision, QRT Tax = Flat Tax. The quantitative ratio tax QRT would revolutionize the tax system. Fiscal Income simplification tax, the ratio of working population and individual income a flat tax measured by ratio of Wages, Salaries, Pensions, less Personal Allowance. The low-income citizens a reduced share of the tax ratio therefore the economy prospers, tax revenues grow, affording increase entrepreneurial incentive in risk taking.

A woodenhead halfwit can find fault:

Corporative QRT-tax based on a designed ratio of Income within the USA and a separate QRT-tax for Global off shore; other than wages, salaries, and pensions. The Corporate tax inherits no deductions for interest payments, dividends, or other forms of payments to the Owners. Income that individuals received from business would have been taxed, the tax QRT would not be involved with income from interest, dividends, or capital gains once deleted. The entire cost of investment plant and equipment would be deducted in the year of purchase. This expeditious deductibility encourages capital formation; more important eliminates bureaucracy and depreciation schedules. QRT Tax = Flat Tax x Total revenue from sales of goods; minus purchases of inputs from other firms. Or you could find a solution!

We need a plan, not finger pointing, it's impolite!

A flat Tax based on Ratio of income, hell that's fair, we are a family, it's called we the people, and our first obligation is America. Pass a bill for a QRT Tax = Flat Tax, everybody pays their fair share, from 5% to whatever 90%! If your income marks below survival, then your exempt, and that 1% Plutocrat can still afford breakfast in Dubai, and my grandkids can go to collage, and inspire a new America in the 21st Century.

The day of derailment:

Behind close doors, the international Hedge Fund Lobbying group, openly stated it would derail the Dodd-Frank bill from existence, Goldman Sachs engaged from within the White House, recruited and enlisted Lobbyist of unlimited resources, they first derailed Elizabeth Warren from ever heading up the defunct bureau of non- financial existence, it's amazing the Lobbyist eliminated the financial funds and derailed the bureau of non- financial existence, they spent billion for loopholes, unlimited

Carried Interest, and I have a suggestion! "Kill the Lobbying system, before they kill us."

Say what!

Guess what! President Obama's professor Elizabeth Warren from Harvard, praised the forth coming new Consumer protection Agency, Elizabeth was to head up the Agency, the President stipulated there was a simple basic rule for the job, that the toaster doesn't blow up in your face, he hired Elizabeth and then fired Elizabeth, two possibilities, the partisan toaster blew up in the Presidents face, or revenge, over a C- Elizabeth Warren gave him as a student.

Ask Phil Gramm, why exclude the SEC?

Congress including the White House passed an omnibus Spending bill in the area of $380-billion, and nobody had the inclination or aptitude to give a damn, when Phil Gramm inserted a 262-page titled Commodity Futures Modernization Act. That excluded the SEC and the Commodity Futures Trading Commission to regulate swaps, protecting financial institutions from overregulation, guess what! The financial Wall Street Lobbyist wrote it. The American Lawmaker's, who you voted for, did not write or understand the terminology of the 262 pages, which was inserted into the bill that became law. And John Dillinger, in 2012 could have just walked into the bank and said please!

Harry S. Truman:

America was not built on fear. America was built on courage, on imagination and an unbeatable determination, to do the job at hand. And President Obama agreed and NASA was downgraded from the budget, subsidies became far more essential for Oil.

The Global BRICs, the day of the Global Lobbyist:

The world population in the year 2012 has exceeded Seven Billion and counting; The resourceful markets for Global Foreign Direct Investment, the FDI is directed towards Global emerging Markets, starting with BRICs the big four Brazil, Russia India and China, the FDI coordinates include Africa, the Middle East, and the Asian markets. America with three hundred and eleven million Americans; will have the distinction of becoming the third most populous country of Global domination. A Plutocratic fraternity of 1% holds the supremacy that dictates over 280 million America's, a pledge that insures the Plutocratic lifestyle of excess. 70% of world growth over the next five years will come from American Conglomerates, as they emerge into the Global markets. The Hoax that unemployment is decreasing, its a fairy tale, the fabrication of numbers afforded deregulation behind close doors, its the Gramm-Leach-Bliley, financial Privacy act. China with twenty percent of the world population, a work force of one Billion three hundred and forty million, the muscle of masses, the American Plutocratic fraternity of elite humanity, understands the value of cheap labor. From a mathematical formula, its classified rock bottom Labor, 1.1 or fewer Taxes, that dictates the demise of 280 Million Americans, denotes Authoritarianism; "The day of the Lobbyist" they have become an authoritative fraternity of Global manipulators. We the people, in five years will become a Caste Society of less than. The revolving door accommodates the Authoritarianism of Global wealth; Wall Street, flexed its authoritative Constitutional boundaries of excess, affording Wall Street's influence to escalate into a Global Market. The lure to arbitrate, an illusion of "we the people," reality it's become a Conglomerate Global monopoly. The entities of Abusive Offshore Tax Schemes are unlimited, hoarding trillions on foreign soil, Foreign trust, foreign partnership with Captive insurance Companies, foreign Corporations and Personal investment Companies, including China's tyrant tail dictating trillions into Global infamy.

Global Market share, the crier of the Lobbyist:

The Lobbyist accentuates a single mindedness of Global monopolization, simply put! The twenty first century, a common denominator, Global Supremacy a single invested bottom line, Global Market share. The Night Stalking Lobbyist cloaked in the cannibalistic lure of deregulation, howling its wares throughout the Congressional halls of influence, the socio-economic solution without adequate health insurance, a pragmatic wonder drug, eliminate Campaign bickering placing the blame elsewhere, when millions of Americans financially can't afford an Education, we are sending our youngest and brightest to die on foreign soil, 2000 died in Afghanistan a thousand and counting this year alone, it's time the fraternity of 1% abstains from devouring the classes, we have citizens that live and die, without ever tasting the sweet smell of opportunity. Wall Street Traders, if not compensated in the millions, will huff and puff and parachute for greener pastures. In reality if your income exceeds 2 million your tax rate should be no less than 90%. A child's anguish, like a weeping sonnet, lost forever in the orator's self-indulgence, no new taxes, you got to be kidding!

Behind Closed Doors, a Plutocratic fraternity:

Forty-six Senate Republicans and two Democrats voted to kill President Barack Obama's $447 Billion spending bill, despite weeks of barnstorming. Majority Republicans oppose a tax surcharge on millionaires starting in 2013 to stimulate the economy; the proposal involved approximately 3% of households. Think about the term abolish the corporate subsidies, that's pure out theft or if you like insanity, if your income exceeds 5 million and you think $120,000 is mind blowing! Try 90%. A Wealthy Welfare mentality, consumes 93 % of the total financial wealth. The "Supreme Court enhanced the Conglomerates arbitration to write tax codes. The Supreme Court determined a Company is a person! I wonder if God ever gave thought to that summation!

9 Trillion, fraudulently deceived:

Wall Street is Bullish on rewarding corporate-ism for capitalism. Zillow's Real Estate tracking company estimated American residential values declined by $9 Trillion, that's theft when Moody and S&P fraudulently deceived, and Wall Street miraculously acquired an additional 412 Billionaires, China ranks second with 115 Billionaires. The financial earnings of American Executives, introduces a troubling inequality for 260 million Americans. The U.S. dollar declined 20 % from 2001. 2.5 % of households make in excess of $400,000 a year, and both Houses bickering over the welfare of the wealthy, in the form of bailouts, while deficit spending became the burden of 260 million Americans. A point of Ratio an average shopper pays $ 3.30 cent for a pound of ground hamburger on sale, the wealthy pays 11.40 for a pound of ground hamburger, because they can afford to flaunt inflation.

Learn from the past:

Afghanistan, Alexander the Great and Russia departed without a whimper or victory, its a war for Conglomerate profit, and the American death count in the summer of 2012 will escalate into the thousands, our young brave American lives are being squandered for political campaign manipulation. Blackwater and Xe-Services are the biggest beneficiaries. Yet the Media and Legislators, men of wisdom, proclaim without military presence, we become venerable, we have two nuclear subs that can eliminate all of humanity.

The Tea Party on conservative:

Say what! John A. Boehner including the Republican pact summoned Wall Street lobbyists, conservative political activists, J.P. Morgan Securities, Goldman Sachs, Google, Citigroup, Bank of America, Wells Fargo, R. J. Reynolds and the list is endless, to Capitol Hill, behind close doors formed a strategy session. The majority contributed individual checks, for the future Speaker. Mr. Boehner took the Norquist pledge! Mr. Boehner! Stated the Republican majority would oppose any tax increases; his insightful reasoning it would weaken the economy, and throw Americans out of work. That's a fraudulent tale of tragedy, 8.3 million unemployed Americans that's a Norquist pledge of Political expediency.

The Myth:

2011 August 1, Both Houses played Chicken little with a sense of partisan fortitude, Speaker of the House Mr. Boehner emerged clutched in partisan rectitude, proclaimed, "4.4 trillion must be reduced without taxing the wealthy," an inflection of determination Mr. Boehner stated, "I'd rather die first!"

Global reform, the plight of the vote:

The bounty of duplicity lingers without a whisper of consequence, financial obligation, transfers the commitment from, "we the people," when in truth, Wall Street Lobbyist write the briefs; that expedites America's deficits, loopholes and subsidies while China is building America's infrastructure from San Francisco to New York. Guess what, that sounds like a Global conspiracy! "Congress auctioned America to the highest bidder."

Believe it!

China State Construction Engineering Group (CSCEC) surpassed our American homegrown giant Bechtel. World Bank, in 2009 blacklisted China's CSCEC for five years for outright bribery and Political Lobbying. In the United States CSCEC construction is building a 4,000-room casino in Atlantic City. In New York, China has won contracts to renovate the subway system, build a new metro platform near Yankee stadium, and refurbish the Alexander Hamilton Bridge over the Harlem River. San Francisco-Oakland bridge; made and constructed in China with inferior steel. The Lobbyist have procured contracts without limitations, including apartment blocks from Washington DC to New York. We pay 22% to export; China pays 2% to import! Thanks to our Legislator's, China and Asia have become, America's number one banking deficit.

From New York To Florida:

A plutocratic Lobbying system derives with the Legislative seal of Global legitimacy. The Lobbyist, a conglomerate force with Global Political Muscle to pursue multibillion-dollar projects. KT Lim, Chairman of one of the wealthiest gambling Conglomerates arrived in America with 500 Billion in pocket change, "Genting is the Asian name of the game!" Lim created an advocacy group known as the New York Gaming Association, at the helm the influential lobbyist, James Featherstonhaugh of New York, hired Bradley Tusk, who was Mayor Bloomberg's campaign manager, New York Gov. Andrew

M. Cuomo proposed legalizing the industry, according to New York Lobbying records they hired Patricia Lynch, a past executive aide to the Democratic Assembly speaker Sheldon Silver, and New Yorks infamous Nicholas A. Spano, former Republican State Senator. After billion invested Mr. Cuomo announced Genting's plans for a $4 billion expansion at Aqueduct the expansion includes three Hotels accommodating an excess of 3,000 rooms including the worlds largest convention center with gambling accommodations.

Guess what's lyrical Genting!

Headlines! "Genting," popped up in Miami, and announced, they plan to build the worlds largest casino on the lyrical Biscayne Bay with 5,200 hotel rooms, 50 restaurants, luxury shops, a convention center, that includes a rooftop lagoon. Guess what! It was not legal for them to build a casino, but Genting spent 400 million anyway on the land, joined the civic association of persuasion, contributed $628,320 to both Republicans and Democrats, and did the right thing, hired two dozen admiring Lobbyist. Guess what! The State Senate panel was overwhelmed; they now have approved not one, not two, but three Mega Casino Resorts in southern Florida. Go figure! "Genting," being a relatively unknown Asian company understands the value of the Lobbyist, weather it's in fifty State or Global! "More than anything else these days, Lobbyist rules, money talks." American's better acquire short order cooking attributes, the Asians love fried rice. Pay back is a bitch!

Goldman Sacks Quarterback, Jester maybe!

Goldman Sachs 10 billion disbursed TARP was returned without a ruffle, you ask why? "Goldman Sachs received 12.9 Billion from AIG in full face value insurance.

The treasury Department "point man" for AIG was Don Jester, an ex employee of guess who! Goldman Sachs, he was overseeing AIG crisis, can you believe that!

Believe it! Goldman Sachs received full value, recommended by Jester, who never mentioned or supported a discounted value. Considering the circumstances, why would he! Timothy Geithner during the chaotic 2008 insanity was head of the Federal Reserve Bank of New York spoke with Jester and Treasury Secretary Hank Paulson besides being overwrought, I figure they where conversing about Don Jester's involvement, for he was working as an outside contractor rather than an official employee, therefore guess what, he was exempt from conflict of Interest, Checkmate, without intent!

Goldman Sachs Global, into the Unknown:

Goldman Sachs rules the Universe by the proposition, "Our clients' interests always come first." Engaging by excellence of Global influence, Mr. Carney Executive Director for thirteen years, his Global position of influence extended from London, Tokyo, New York, that includes all the industrialized nations, Goldman Sachs inner circle a pattern of Global domination emerges from Mario Draghi governor of the European Central

Bank, Mario Monti Italian Prime mister, Australia, China, Japan, and directly to the White House personal. Hank Paulson, Lloyd Blankfein Mark Patterson, Timothy Geithner, Gary Gensler, Robert Hormats, Joshua Bolten, Jon Corzine and the list is endless. A New World Order or a Conspiracy of the first Order! From Presidents, Chancellors, Prime Ministers and Dictators.

Sachsism! Aggressively toxic, astutely perceptive, sophisticated with an imperious responsibility of politically connected Globally. March 14, 2012 Goldman Sachs Executive Director Greg Smith; resigned after 12 years, he stated, "I can honestly say that the environment now is as toxic and destructive as I have ever seen it, I have seen five different managing directors refer to their own clients as muppets!"

Congress needs to understand the difference between domestic and a feral cat of Global intent. The Plutocratic domestication has become a feral cat of Global domination, and America has become a financial burden.

So be it!

CHAPTER FOUR

From the 19th Century a Max Muller quote:

"Would not the child's heart break in despair when the first cold storm of the world sweeps over it, if the warm sunlight of love from the eyes of mother and father did not shine upon him like the soft reflection of divine light and love?"

The three branches of Government, Executive, Legislative and Judicial are the eyes of Mother and Father. The president nor his Cabinet nor Congress or the Supreme Court reflected the divine light onto, "We the people"

Congress wears blinders:

J.P. Morgan Chase & Co. it's an American multinational banking corporation of securities, investments and retail, including one of the largest Hedge Funds in the United States, sold fraudulent rated Toxic subprime mortgages throughout the world, they where fined 150 million and nobody was charged with fraud, AIG, Goldman Sacks, Lehman Brothers, Morgan Stanley and my favorite Bank of America busted the financial Real Estate trillion dollar bubble, and bankruptcy became the cry, "nobody was going to jail! So pass out the bonus. Congress has yet to regulate Wall Street or its Toxic practices." NASA by the end of 2012 will be only a memory that provided over 13 hundred innovative tools for industry and Science. It's a mathematical reality tax the 1% 90% till they pay off the deficit. Our educated youth understands loan deficit, they are obligated till the hereafter.

A Soldier's Foreclose, while dying for his country:

J.P. Morgan Chase, illegally overcharged 6,000 active combat military personnel and refused to admit any wrong doing, then add a dose of insult, the bank, I don't give a damn; illegally foreclosed an excess of military homes without a patriotic thought. It required a class action suit before they settled for 27 million in compensation. It proves if you ask how to honor American fighting men and women, try legal action and foreclosure, and the bravest of our young got screwed and committed suicide for serving their country!

J.P. Morgan Chase paid 2 billion in fines for financing Enron; J. P. Morgan Chase helped underwrite 15.4 billion of WorldCom's bonds they coughed up another 2 billon. The list goes beyond arrogance or the poem by Marina Tsvetaeva, "I know the only truth! The others- cast aside!" And no man should have to serve four tours without appreciation and recognition, the truth, we cast aside our youth for Political achievement.

A moment for the fallen, for they are cast aside:

Three days of silence, President Obama's tribute to the demise of 30 American Hero's that gave the ultimate sacrifice, President Obama orated the words "extraordinary sacrifices," his statement was a political keynote of sincerity, "a reminder of "extraordinary sacrifices," they who died alongside their comrades, in pursuit of a hopeful future. Thousands came home in the dark of night, draped over their casket an American flag; the bells should have tolled, for the fallen, they are the cherished and sacred, without recognition, we have become cowards, for its our children that made the warrior's ultimate sacrifice. The Mothers prayer, a memory, that proclaimed the untold silence, a moment of a warrior's life. A Chinook helicopter, became the legend, of an irreversible finality, in a province where death tolled thirty, a recipient prose, a warrior's mettle of brotherhood, forever bears witness to the tragedy of Wardak, for now the youngest and our bravest, belong to that Warrior's fraternity, the embodiment of ultimate sacrifice. The rhythm distance a single bugle cadence of sacrifice, for they have risen, awaiting their call to duty. They are the very essence of genesis, the Warrior's oblation to country.

Obama Inaugural address, January 2009:

"Today I say to you that the challenges we face, are real. They are serious and they are many. They will not be met easily or in a short span of time. But know this, America - they will be met. On this day, we gather because we have chosen hope over fear, unity of purpose over conflict and discord." Let's face the facts he never said he would balance the budget. His speech had the abrupt interpretation of General Mac Arthur's departure from Corregidor Island in 1942, except the General did return. My question, will President Obama return for a second term? Yes! That's if Mitt is the Republican candidate running for President, he's detached from reality, he doesn't know a doughnut from a hole in the ground, he wanted that chocolate thing with a round hole in the middle he asked, "what's it called!"

President Obama a Lobbyist in the White House!

"I don't take a dime, of their money, and when I am president, they won't find a job in my White House." He should have listened to Andrew Jackson; "Unless you become more watchful in your status and check the spirit of the exclusive privileged, you will in the end find that... control over America's interests has passed into the hands of the 1 % Plutocrats." It's called a Lobbyist inside the White House with a Waiver, or it's a short walk to deregulation. Reality is a bitch if you lose your Presidency or your pen! So far the Republicans are determined to keep you in office for 4 more years. I got a suggestion tell the American Voter, that anybody that excels 10 million will be taxed 90% till the deficit is eliminated. I would tell the voter anybody who took the Norquist pledge, vote for an independent Congressman or Senator. Our infrastructure is our first financial obligation, tells Congress to take a 10% cut in pay! Hell and Education will freeze over first!

How do you count the lobbyist in the Hen house?

Obama's presidential order restricting lobbyists inside the chicken coop, that's a neat trick with a revolving door and a Conglomerate hawk circling the legislative abbey, the problem there are more Lobbyist than legislators' and most of them are forth right Ex-Senators and Congressmen converts, or in truth turncoats. The term containment should pertain to all legislators, a three-year hiatus from Committee operational participation. Ex Legislative personal are afforded to participate in areas that are restricted to the public, a question of contention, Insider Trading and Insider manipulation should be classified outright graft. President Obama's administration close door influence has become the institution of "the Conglomerates Hen House". The key difference pertains to privy; it has the distinction along with death, no intent or obligation to reform.

Try double-talking intent:

I kid you not!" 2010 created a group of Lobbyist from both Houses and introduced an Investigation Committee to inform the public of its intent. Now that's the art of double-talking beyond ones own ability to decipher.

The Investigation Committee in its wisdom said, "We will benefit by the experience of our predecessors. This inquiry will enhance our ability to serve the public interest, a predetermined agenda must be based on careful research, and therefore we cannot afford to bog down in partisan infighting!" It's beyond one's ability to decipher; the Phantom Lobbyist predetermined agenda to influence behind close doors. You might think that procedure would be considered a conflict of our Democratic interest. The Supreme Court said privacy was their constitutional right!   Tom DeLay Republican from Texas was prompted to resign over a particular scandal, except Robert Ney Republican from Ohio, pleaded guilty and was sentenced to 30 months in prison. Tom Delay did the honorable thing and became a Lobbyist.

Influence peddling; a war chest of millions in tact:

A Senator converting to Lobbyist, guess what! If he's Considering a Career change the necessity becomes influence peddling that requires a war chest of millions in tact, without a doubt it has an inspiring ability to reap the perks. Northrop Grumman was Lobbying to retain a 35 billion dollar air force contract for plane re-fuelling. Now Ex Senator Lott with a sizzling hot to trout 1. 3 million War Chest, came aboard with title Vice President, contributed to Senator Saxby Chambliss and Roger Wicker's cause, a functional significance for they both sat on the Senate Armed Service Committee. Do you have to ask!

That's sounds suspect:

It took exactly one week for Senator's Byron Dorgan of North Dakota and Bob Bennett of Utah to become Lobbyist on the famous K street; they are now senior policy advisers for a Washington, DC Lobbyist law firm. The Ex Legislators are heading for K Street, with war chest funds in tact.

As the world turns subsidies flow:

Patton Boggs, the largest federal lobbying firm announced that it acquired Breaux-Lott Leadership Group, a strategic subterfuge of partisan influence from former Senators John Breaux, Democrat of Louisiana, and Trent Lott, Republican of Mississippi.

Lobbyist Trent Lott converted to embracing inspirational, for big Oil! He's against solar energy, the hell with clean air, it's just to damn expensive, and the sun doesn't shine where he lives.

The Lobbyist AEF Drill baby drill!

America's Energy Future, what a great Seminar titled Oil! John Breaux, Trent Lott, Jeremy Rifkin, John Hofmeister, and

Gene Randall, perpetuated the necessity for Oil subsidies. The Town Crier, Lobbyist John Breaux voted yes twice, once for Oil drilling on national security grounds, and the second time voted yes, on defunding solar energy. "Let the Subsidies flow! Drill baby drill!

Inducements and subsidies:

BP third quarter profits total 4.9 billion earnings, Louisiana Democrat Mary Landrieu banked almost $17,000 from the oil giant for her war chest voted not to repeal subsidies. The world of Legislative insanity, BP coughed up 7 billion from the twenty billion regarding the Gulf of Mexico oil spill, except they claimed 9.9 billion taxation a credit from the disaster. The Internal Revenue under federal law cannot discuss the issue. The Internal Revenue Service is the last frontier of legitimacy; they can't be bribed, but somebody sure as hell can, they call it subsidies not bribery. 40,000 New York City individuals, are homeless, they call subsidizing them Socialism.

Exxon Mobil third quarter profits 10.3 billion, Exxon Mobil gave the max contribution to Scott Brown campaign before he voted not to repeal subsidies. 8.2 % Americans are unemployed and each day the pangs of less than, grows. Executive Rex Tillerson 141th on the Forbes 2011, total compensation, and $ 28,952,558.00 was taxed below the 15%. A 100 to 5 bet, Exxon Mobil third quarter will exceed the highest third quarter in their history, regardless of the price of oil per barrel. Chevron third quarter profits $7.83 billion, total earnings;

Chevron gave Brown $5000 two weeks before he voted not to repeal subsidies. Royal Dutch Shell third quarter profits 6.98 billion, total earnings for 2011 through the third quarter 21 billion. Don't ask if they contributed, of course they did! Conoco Phillips third quarter $2.62 billion total earnings for 2011 through the third quarter $9 billion, Conoco Phillips gave Brown $1000 two weeks before he voted not to repeal subsidies.

Oil Lobbyist with a formula:

Try eliminating subsidies, believe it or not, the Lobbyist have a subsidies formula, $D(p_c) = S(p_c + t)$ Algebraically, the bottom line if the government eliminates subsidies, the Oil Industry Algebraically will raise gas price, without a barrel of hesitation the Lobbyist introduced "The Case of depleted crude," If cost rates decline the recipients may decide to produce less crude. In effect, the Oil Conglomerates will find the Global market an inducement for off shore labor and tax benefits. GE Oil is strategizing a refinery in China. CBO's Congressional budget office deficit for fiscal year 2012, $1.2 trillion is a $93 billion increase, over projection. Try eliminating subsidies. Congress said I don't think so! Obligation is an unforgiving financial bitch.

Converting the Wall Street beast:

The Infamous Four, the Ex-Majority Leaders from upper and lower House have relocated. Senator Trent Lott, Senator Bob Doyle, and former House majority leaders Richard A.

Gephardt, Dick Armey and an additional 125 Ranking Staffers maintain their revolving door influence between Capital Hill and K Street; it's that financial cozy homelike atmosphere of Ranking Staffers that turned Lobbyist, where limited access to Congress, became a predicament! Behold the mythical world of Legislative ability. They simply reclassified the Ranking Staffers from Lobbyist to Legislative privileged consultants!

A twist, that's a Lobbyist inside the hen house."

Four out of five Staffers that left Capital Hill registered with one of Washington's Lobbying firms, or an independent Lobbyist for a Conglomerate. As the world turns, exodus the title Lobbyist, a transformation into legislative privileged Staffer, they converted their Lobbyist badge and crossed the revolving door of Capital Hill with the legislative title privileged Staffer.   That's a political metamorphosis in reverse, if you quack and have feathers, your still a turncoat Lobbyist.

What came first the lobbyist or legislative Staffers:

Congress rules over Ethics, 150 Lobbyist have moved into Capital hill lock stock and influence, they are legally designated as privileged Staffers for members of Congress and House committees. They advocate and write legislation in sync with interest pertaining to their association with lobbying firms. What's in a name Peter Haller, alias Peter Simonyi, the former Goldman Sachs VP now Staffer Peter Haller working for Chairman

Darrell Issa Republican House Oversight Committee to block regulations and coordinate efforts to advocate advantage to Goldman Sachs, that simply is the bottom line. Abramoff would indicate, without intent that's not corruption, for it's not a breach of Legislative Ethics, or is it! Not according to Congress. How you spell corruption, privileged without intent!

The Goldman corridors:

Public records show Patterson worked as a lobbyist for Goldman Sachs in 2008. The Chickens are still kicking up the gravel, former U.S. Fed chief Alan Greenspan and past Treasury Secretary Hank Paulson and Vice President Peter Simonyi are still cackling around the hen house. In reality your vote has a shelf life of thirty days past the swearing in ceremony.

The first amendment has become the Plutocratic fraternity, a 1% Society of Congressional Conglomerates redress of deregulation and tax loopholes. To hell with the red white and blue, unless of course its tax deductible.

U.S. Senate Chris Coons, Ban former Senators!

Democratic candidate for the U.S. Senate Chris Coons proposed a lifetime ban for members of the Senate who attempt to return to Washington as lobbyist. He was quoted, "When a Senator resigns or defeated, should not be rewarded with high paying lobbying contracts that influence laws, a five-year ban on Senior Staff, and restore balance to the legislative process." Chris Coons is a hero in the trenches, but Congress is not listening. It's no longer a joke! Congress has become the steeping stone of turncoat defectors between Insider Trading and becoming an influence peddler to the highest bidder. Send @ E-mail to Senator Chris Coons, with a simple message, we are listening, ban the turncoats!

HAMP and the on-line scavenger chasers:

On March 4, 2009, the U.S. Department of the Treasury announced the Home Affordable Modification program (HAMP) designated to reduce at-risk borrowers' monthly mortgage payments. Freddie Mac was to implement the program. Now nothing can go wrong, except Bank of America, JP Morgan Chase and Wells Fargo Bank cited President Barack Obama's HAMP as negative and a dismal failure verse and chapter, the key ingredient of disapproval was non profitable. The Treasury Department bellows back, they would not receive payments for loan modifications, first conceive the Banks would participate, except Vultures are feeding on the HAMP carcass, the on-line scavengers are on a eating frenzy, there are more Attorney's handling Bankruptcy under the pretense of affordable mortgage modification. Now on Capital Hill the Republicans are demanding a halt to HAMP and all housing related programs, you got to be kidding, that's better than earmarks, or a pork barbecue, yeah! That's not going to happen. HAMP will expire on December 31, 2012, read the fine print, 31 days delinquent and you qualify, as I said the scavengers are on an eating frenzy!

Earmarks a form of bipartisan into partisan:

Earmarks became the bargaining chips, for the Plutocrats pet projects; it should be reclassified as a partisan's bribery to bipartisan conversion. The title of accuracy is not wasteful spending, it's premeditated "duplicity" that's attributing to Americas future it's called receivership, we have acquired a AA+ credit rating from Standard and Poor's, go to the website, Taxpayers against earmarks, it should create a serious inclination to send your Senator an E-mail. It's not a joke the virus has a partisan affiliation it contaminates both Democrats and Republicans and both Houses.

Pork Barrel appropriation, spend Tax dollars:

The alleged Pork-Barrel project known, as Big Dig was the pride of Tip O'Neal the Speaker of the House of Representatives, Tip relocated 3.5 miles of interstate, with a minor exception it was underground. It ended up costing the American Taxpayer 14.6 billon, that's only a little over 4 billion per mile. They named one of the tunnels after Tip O'Neal, They should have named both tunnels, one Tip 14.6 billion a going and the other O'Neal 22 billion a coming.

Congress Pork, a contradiction in pedigree:

The Pig Book released the world of Pork Barrel

spending revealed 9,129 earmarks worth $16.5 billion illustrates that most members of Congress did not eliminate the submissive practice. Pork Barrel spending is a slavish Congressional genealogy of arm twisting for a vote." An Example $4,841,000 for wood utilization research requested by 13 Senators and 10 Representatives. The research cost taxpayers over $100 million. According to Rep. Chellie Pingree D-Maine, "the benefit from spending100 million, producing better wood composites. Think about it, it's an ingenious way to produce toothpicks, and acquire a bipartisan vote. And the Education system somehow is paying the price in pencils and notebooks, they don't have a sufficient number of teachers left to distribute the wood.

Pork, Potato and Sea Salt a Barbecue without:

Politicians from both parties recognize that taxpayers are seething and incensed with dismissive Pork Barrel spending activities in Washington, Guess what! 2, 573, 000 for potato research in 4 States requested by five Senators and 4 Representatives, for its Washington's holy grail, Potato farmers, sea salt and a partisan vote. "Yet! Kids go to bed without French Fries or sea salt!"

Sometimes you get a bargain:

In 2010 the Pork Barrel was 16.5 billion; Sen. Olympia Snow, Reps. Mike Michaud and Chellie Pingree only requested $200,000 for lobster research at the Maine Department of Marine Resources. What happened to the four lobsters in Quarantine? $206,000 for wool research in Montana that makes no sense, all our wool products comes from China. $1,000,000 for Portsmouth Music Hall, it's in the State of New Hampshire. "We need health Care for our kids and elderly, try playing that tune on your heart strings, of pass the Pork."

Pork Sausage:

There was an old saying in Chicago dead men don't read. In DC they have a saying, nobody reads the Bill, take a Bill pump it full of pork then introduce the "Bill in six volumes of three hundred pages each," Get the picture, that's called stuffing the pork.

Obama promised Kosher not pork!

President Obama said, "no more pork!" Guess what John Mc Cain did? John McCain verbally slashed and gashed President Obama's interpretation of eliminating, "indebted pork!" The bell toiled the message of untruth, the Budget McCain verbalized was enraptured with pork from the heavenly House of Representatives, the emphasis of McCain's statement, "every American should without delay Google endingspending.com. McCain didn't make it out of the box, the fiscal year ending in 2011, skyrocketed an orbit of 39,000 earmarks totaling $130 billion. Do you really think your vote counts, Wall Street Lobbyist control the purse stings that subsides the elections, the answer is of course not!

Two sides of the trough:

$277,000 for potato pest management in Wisconsin [how did you come up with that figure, that only takes care of the paper work, then what?]

$246,000 for bovine tuberculosis in Michigan and Minnesota [Let's get real the test tubes alone, will brake the budget, then what?]

$522,000 for blueberry disease and breeding in New Jersey [that situation has merit for the Jersey Shore.]

$500,000 for oyster safety in Florida [talk to BP they love Tax deductions]

$349,000 for swine-waste management in North Carolina [now that's a porcine crock what part of the swine don't they eat.]

$413,000 for peanut research in Alabama [ask Jimmy Carter he's got the nuts.]

$247,000 for virus free wine grapes in Washington [try a food program for the unemployed, have you checked the price of grapes.]

$208,000 beaver management in North Carolina [you got to be dam well kidding or your brother-in-law needs work.]

$94,000 for blackbird management in Louisiana [send them to Texas they will be happy to enlighten them.]

$165,000 for maple syrup research in Vermont [sweeten the pot with less and pay the Educators.]

$235,000 for noxious weed management in Nevada [that's not the only thing noxious in Nevada, try eliminating pork.]

$100,000 for the Edgar Allen Poe Cottage Visitor's Center in New York [sell T-shirts, like every body else.]

$300,000 for the Polynesian Voyaging Society in Hawaii [sell bikinis on the sea shore.]

The list goes on and on, and in their wisdom they decided to cut Education. Pork Barrel and earmark projects, are attached to the federal budget by members of the appropriation committees, that of the United States Congress and future Lobbyist.

The privileged few:

Thomas Jefferson defined the written law must pertain equal to every individual person, regardless of position or stature, Our Bill of Rights should be considered an accurate representation that secures all Americans equal civil responsibilities. Therefore a criminal act of indiscretion should bear equal justice for all! The reality, it's dependent on the stature of privileged, equality it's the most inalienable ethical responsibility of all human rights. The Bill of Rights accurately defined, are God given by our forefathers sacrifice, without absolution or exemption for the privileged, Inside trading that's a criminal act, no where in the Constitution does it exempt any Senator Or Congressman from Insider Trading. Earmarks, Pork the hallmark of the affluent should be eliminated from passage of financial impetus to influence a nay or yea vote! Wall Street has transformed into a Global Universe with a single loyalty, financial bounty! The Lobbyist tool of financial persuasion, determines the benefit of the affluent. Can you pilfer, abscond and surreptitiously alter the first amendment from we the people to Wall Street.

The Day of the Lobbyist:

A Congressional distinction between Lobbyist and Shakespeare's Sonnet 29, it's the fortune of the deaf without conscious, a Lobbyist sings hymns at heaven's gate for intemperance possessed above the boundaries of faithful service. Wall Street's financial campaign funds exceeded 1.7 billion. Dodd Frank's Wall Street Reform Act, implemented by Congress, signed by President Obama, invoked an inspirational conspiracy by Congress, Simply put Dodd Frank's Reform Act was not financially accessible!

A decade of access:

Private Jets, unlimited junkets into the world of extravagance, from St. Andrews to Dubai, luxury suites exceeding 20,000 per night, freebees redundant beyond the Constitutional limit of expectable, and palm greasing summoned the Constitutional Commandment, for the select few!

Jack Abramoff Lobbyist in name alone, a self-portrayal reprehensible was the grasp of addiction, the opium phantom possessed a theatrical status of Political bearing, an allusion. Cloaked by altruism, benevolence dispensing millions, translated without disclosure, in the real world, corruption would only apply to the masses, "we the people." Once upon our National honor was national property of the highest value

A time to remember:

The siege of stagnation dictated the rule; the ferret depth of fraud was Record March 9, 1933. The Seventy-Third Congress First Session exposed the deception perpetrated through use of Federal Reserve Bank Notes. America sixty-six years later simply forgot, yet that memory has never faltered from my impressionable viscera of a generation's desperation, which consumed them without a prayer or God. The Plutocratic 1% that year traveled to Europe and sent their kids to Harvard.

The big three:

The three branches of Government, Executive, Legislative and Judicial are the eyes of Mother and Father. The president nor his Cabinet nor Congress or the Supreme Court reflected the divine light onto, "We the people." First your voice must be heard then your vote.

"So be it!"

CHAPTER FIVE

Mot's portrayal of America:

The neighborhood kids strolled in the back door,

without a question or thought, for permission was waylaid by a famished whim of what ever, an abrupt rasping shrill, "Hey! Is any body home," that unholy squeal divulged a neighborhood rug rat prowling for food, "is that fish, I smell frying," the aroma of fried something or another from afar lingered its lure of invite, would inquire with an amble stroll of intruders boldness would assume a kitchen pose with sleeves rolled up a hand placed firmly on the table with elbows exposed, inquired, "tell me the truth, what's –a-frying!" The American flag waved prominently by the count, four to the average block. Clattering hoofs, was a common sound of day and time, it indicated Buski the Iceman's prompt arrival, he was Polish, with broken English he revealed a kaput sense of alien humor, forearms chiseled, exposed mind boggling reddish blue letters, with a chopped up snake, boldly illuminated the message, don't tread on me! A hundred pound block of ice with a single stroke, converted into two fifty-pound blocks as one floated upward onto Buski's shoulder to a vocal rendition, "Wislica!" I vant to see Wislica, in snowy time," he always removed the tray of melted ice, from the bottom of the Icebox with a sense of achievement, he would collect twenty-five cents, cash on delivery, he was an independent. And we kids would steal ice chips from his wagon and run for our lives, screaming Wislica!

Mr. Joseph Hess was strictly down to business; insurance was the name of his game, Joseph always had a new program with a three color chart depicting the additional benefits for an extra 90 cents a month you could have a private hospital room which included a menu and a portable radio from the standard two-bed room of 5.50. Mr. Hess collected on the first Monday of each month like clockwork. 9:15 prompt was the tap on our front screen door. With his pencil and tattered payment book in hand, he would go down the list; Hospital, Car, Life Retirement and Insurance plan, and every week he would pencil in each cost separate and then out loud he would add up the total sum. My mother would flip open the monthly payment folder to the Insurance compartment, where neatly set up amounts due, first the one dollar bills then the change, to which his exact words, always ended the same way, Well Irene stay healthy, and god willing, I will see you the first of next month. The milkman was the egg man; he collected on Friday morning, the amount due was neatly wrapped and placed into the neck of an empty milk bottle. We had an Icebox until the spring of 39 when the electric refrigerator became reliable to a degree of acceptance, and the world became unreliable, so we simply locked our doors, and somehow our neighbors became like the two party system cynically worlds apart.

"1930 National honor of the highest value, jobs."

The Empire State Building became the great American sprit. John J. Raskob masterminds a beacon of grandeur, during the Great Depression the worlds tallest phenomenon, John simply asked William Lamb the architect, "William, can you guarantee that it will not fall down?" It became the seventh wonder of the modern world, King Kong's swan song!

The Empire State building was completed on May 1, 1931, the cost was a staggering four hundred thousand a floor, and total cost 41 million. It required a work force of 3,400 individuals, 1 year and 45 days including Saturdays and Sundays to complete the project, equated 7 million man-hours, with the loss of six lives.

President James Monroe, March 4, 1817, at his first inaugural address articulated, "National honor is national property of the highest value." One hundred and fourteen years latter, American held its breath as Hoover's index finger illuminated 1,250 feet of American greatness of the highest value into the twenty-century. King Kong and Fay Wray in the 1933 production turned the Empire State Building into the number one tourist attraction. "National honor is national property of the highest value."

Edgar Allan Poe quote:

"The true genius shudders at incompleteness - and usually prefers silence to saying something which is not everything it should be." That's not a politician, for he surely can talk from both sides of his mouth, with or without a sane thought as long as it's complimented by placing the blame elsewhere.

Political insight, "say Social what!" 1935:

It's amazing how the Political arena evolves from desperation to divine intervention when it becomes a campaign promise of dismissal. Social programs in the scheme of equality must inherit the necessity of "we the people." for the season of equality. Our forefathers fought and died for life, liberty and the pursuit of happiness, with Heroic reflection for heritage it's "We the people!" Yet a Plutocratic 1% fraternity has indoctrinated the Slave masters mentality, set your mind right, boy!

The federal program created by the Social Security Act of 1935 had divorced women and non-white women were excluded from Social Security benefits. That was an acceptable reality as adoption shackled a racist thorn on "illegitimate" priority by pedigree; America presented an untold abundance of lost souls, the year 1935. I was one of those lost souls, except I didn't know it! My life by misfortune was not predestined; I emerged from the dearth of an illegitimate nonexistence, into officialdom by the fourteenth amendment where precedence was deemed. I had no earthly concept that I was flawed inside a Bureaucratic stopgap of diddlysquat, with a shattering four forms in order to be reclassified.

September 1939, Hitler invades Poland:

The first day of September Germany attacked Poland, September 27,Warsaw surrenders, I asked, "how in hell did Germany achieve such an overwhelming victory," my father responded, "Germany had 2,000 Tanks, 1,000 planes, and 40 infantry divisions. On the other hand Poland had 11 cavalry brigades, it was an impressive display of white horses charging a thousand tanks."

Russia invaded Finland and Germany signed, "The pact of Steel," with non other than Mussolini, the Pope prayed. England declares war on Germany and America sends military aid to England, but Roosevelt demands to stays neutral. Earthquake kills 30,000 in Chili, and Hitler kills 60,000 non-desirables for openers.

On the home front staying neutral:

The Social Security act mails out its first checks in 1939 to the elderly. Gold priced at 35.00 dollars an ounce speculation gold will soar in 1940, the following day Gold loses fifty cents an ounce.

Unemployment holding an impressive 18% and the thunder gathering of war clouds were over England, and Mussolini attacked Ethiopia for effect. America demands to stay neutral. DuPont introduced a synthetic fiber that gave birth to the nylon and Benny Goodman set the world into "Swing" and America was ready to boogie not fight. Persia said what the hell, let's change our image and became Iran, go figure. Hitler made his declaration that he wanted peace and invaded Poland, France flexed its muscle and gave Hitler an ultimatum, "desist or face the consequences", I figured the part about desist was what pissed Hitler off, that's when the SS occupied France it was a perfect sunny day in June, 1940. The Nazis bombed Coventry, England and World War Two became the Big Deal.

It's amazing about the influence of bias:

In 1939 Jon Nance Garner was Vice President of the United States and plastic was also an unknown commodity, the KKK was on a decline and twice as deadly. Hitler's Mein Kamp became politically the new bible, he altered the sixth Commandment, and thou shall not kill from the consciousness for expediency, therefore replacing humanity for genocide. Henry Ford's Model T sold in the millions, he didn't invent but introduced the assembly line into the industry; he was Anti Semitic and openly praised Hitler for his degrading the Jews. And yet eleven percent of his work force where blacks earning five dollars a day twice the average pay scale. My point most people are selectively bigoted for their own imperfections, my bias lies within my own shortcomings.

The demand to stay neutral remained in tact:

October 29, 1940, President Roosevelt, radio address the Selective Service Act of 1940, a silent hush lingered, an authoritative timbre trumpeted forth with conviction, "our democratic army has existed for one purpose only; the defense of our freedom!" President Roosevelt paused knowing his political existence was in the balance of neutrality, caution related a sense, yet loomed the chatter of war and national security. "There can be no appeasement, with ruthlessness! We must be the great army of Democracy." The Country rattled its discontent towards the draft, demanding that Roosevelt stay neutral. Roosevelt's fireside chat forged an anxiety of resentment, the battle cry; we don't want our babies going to war. Roosevelt was strategizing the master scheme, for survival became an incontestable reality, whatever path infamy must take.

The Lend-Lease Act of 1941:

In January 1941, Franklin D. Roosevelt was busier than a possum indoctrinating the country that war clouds where just around the corner, and sacrifice was in full swing. Great Britain was no longer finically able to procure billion for arms. America was semi aware that Hitler was becoming the Great War Monger and it was no longer England's problem to solve.

Then on January 6, 1941, Roosevelt asked Congress for the authority to supply arms to Great Britain and including other nations, his words echoed forth, "We cannot, and we will not, tell Great Britain that they must surrender, merely because of present inability to pay for the weapons which we know they must acquire."

The opposition was fierce, Aviation Hero Colonel Charles A. Lindbergh with obstinacy stood before the House Foreign Affairs Committee, expressed an abusive vilification that American influence was for war profiteering. Lindberg protested with conviction that it would directly embroil America into the war, and Germany would defeat the United States. Lindbergh was extremely vocal about staying natural and Roosevelt was well aware that the Gallup poll proclaimed that 83% of Americans were against the war.

Isolationists, Senator Hamilton Fish, Senator Dewey Short and Senator Karl Mundt of the house Foreign Affairs openly opposed lend lease, Congressional internationalists supported Roosevelt, as Representative James Wadsworth expressed it, "startling!" he expressed the powers that the President would posses where enormous. After weeks of intense debate, the House voted 265 to 165 to approve the measure. In March 1941, President Franklin D. Roosevelt signed the Lend-Lease Act—that authorized Roosevelt to lease, or lend military arms to any country that designated as vital to American national security.

The United States delivered to Russia lend lease from June 1941 through September 1945, paid for in Gold. Even after the war Charles A. Lindbergh refused to reject his pre-war assessment of Germany, "History is full of its misuse. There is no better example than Nazi Germany". Lindbergh affectionately maintained his status as the "Lone Eagle."

1941 Ambassador Wadsworth was Assistant Industrial Relations Manager of the Aircraft Division of the Curtiss-Wright Corporation. The Lobbyist influence was in full swing, the Navy awarded Curtis-Wright 125 million for its Ohio plant. Senator Harry S. Truman found the Ohio plant was shipping defective engines, Harry was quoted years later, "I sent a couple of generals, to Leavenworth, and I believe they are still there. President Truman said, "I don't give a damn if it was with or without intent"

The great debate of Pearl Harbor:

The headline - Japan Bombs Pearl Harbor: The article was published by the editors of Legacy Publishing July in 1941 five months before infamy.

On November 26,1941 Washington ordered all US aircraft carriers, the Enterprise, Hornet, Saratoga, Langley and the Lexington, out of Pearl Harbor. The same day Cordell Hull issued a document demanding the Japanese withdrawal from Indochina and China. U.S. Naval Intelligence called, "The document the mark of war."

The infamous telegram sent on November 30,1941 was not ignored the alert sounded for battle stations, an impressive no show of the Japanese military might. Then a week later the infamous December 7, Telegram arrived and guess what! It was ignored and placed into the Monday pick up box, yet nobody questioned the fact that the United States Pacific Aircraft Carrier fleet was not at Pearl Harbor. History proved it required an act of infamy before, FDR declared war with Germany and Japan.

The day of declaration Pearl Harbor:

December 8, 1941, President Roosevelt, declares war between the United States and Japan. Germany declares war on the United States. America was ready to fight, the House rushed through a declaration of war in less than an hour.
Congresswoman Jeannette Rankin's opposition at roll call was anticipated, they refused to allow her to articulate her view on the floor, she was shunned until roll call, "As a woman, I can't go to war," she exhaled with verbal determination, "and I refuse to send anyone else. My vote no!" contempt erupted with a rupture of overflowing booing. Rankin throughout the war accused Roosevelt of instigating the attack on Pearl Harbor without support; She was shunned throughout the war by the press and the public. Sixty years later California Democrat Congresswoman Barbara Lee stood alone defending her conviction in opposition to authorize military intervention against terrorism, she had public praise, for her single minded conviction. What a day makes, plus sixty years.

America is ready to fight:

1941 Germany launches attack in the Balkans. Yugoslavia surrenders, Nazi tanks enter Athens; Hitler invades Russia in June the weather was picture perfect. The Atlantic Charter commenced August14; things at this point where moving on the fast track, FDR and Churchill agree on war aims, lend lease and America will fight. Japanese attacks Philippines and Guam, the news reel depicted genocide beyond the concept of butchery as women and children where bayoneted in full view of the world, without a thought of compassion, that was the straw that altered our determination for survival, we are enlisting by the droves, Germany and good old Italy declare war on the United States and Congress declares war on the whole damn bunch, that was on December 11,1941. I'll never forget that day, because a Wise Guy from my neighborhood, Tony Cabazoni who sold hot merchandise out of the trunk of his car, his presentation [pitch] was an original, "buy one get the second one for half price, I never thought of Tony as a true blue patriot, but to my surprise, Tony sold his business, joined the Marines that very week, the reality popped an impression on my way of thinking, America was Tony's home and he was proud to fight for his Country, and his convictions, yet he was still a Wise Guy, by the end of 1944 Tony a high school drop out, had two purple hearts, two silver stars and Captain bars he was proud of being a Marine more so than a Wise Guy.

1942 brought forth W.W. Two and mayhem:

War clouds where brewing over Europe, and my core of existence, was a crystal radio set inside a cigar box, I constructed that crystal radio with pains taking self-doubt and considerable difficulty, from my youthful prospective saying wireless without an electric plug or batteries was an overrated idiots pipe dream, I surmised with an insightful knowledge that I had spent one dollar and a quarter for which I received a little magic crystal, and directions, I could not conceive a Cat's Whisker Receiver, without batteries or a power source, I read the instructions six or seven times, and the only comforting assessment was the merciful message at the bottom of the page, stating in bold black print, required time less than an hour for completion, a deceitful misconception, I arrived at the final obstacle three hours and twenty minuets latter, it was a learning curve of my stupidity, I ultimately grasped the term grounded, silence surpassed my lack of self-confidence, then came the glorious moment of achievement; the miracle was my finger dexterity sliding the pointer over the tuning coil, a high pitched voice articulated the pleasure of smoking Luck Strikes. I alone had discovered the greatest intervention of the twenty-century; the miracle surpassed Moses and the parting of the red Sea, all encompassed inside a Cuban Havana cigar box and my world war two headset a gift from Curtis LeMay, whom I never meet personally, unknowingly participated in my cunning plot of silently invisibility, an adolescent restriction known as nine-o'clock curfew. Army Air Force Brigadier General Curtis E. LeMay, lovingly known as Old Iron Pants, gave my Father a genuine sheep covered headset with his name stenciled inside the headband, they meet in March of 42 in Salt Lake City Utah at the time I believe he was a full bird Colonel, my father was with the OSS training pilots on survival techniques, during a drinking session, my father got around to mentioning he had a son Mot, yours truly, and related I was somewhat beyond the normal of being a patriot regarding the war effort, because of my age I had settled for donating my Saturdays as a Boy Scout packaging bandages for the Red Cross instead of killing Germans. The next day, Old Iron Pants presented my father with my infamous genuine sheep covered headset, affording my total silent concealment, to awake at 2am with a fanaticism to indulge my appetite with a wide range of insightful adult programs, the Shadow, Night Beat, Mystery Theater, Cloak and Dagger, Lights Out, Suspense and Inner Sanctum, all took second place to Patton and the war, I swear old blood and guts was moving faster than grease lightning. From my point of view George S. Patton was my nightly Superman, I followed his escapades from the day he arrived in North Africa, Sicily and Lorrain that's where his tanks ran out of gas, Eisenhower really irked me off, when he transferred Patton's supplies to Montgomery for operation Market Garden, I went insane over Eisenhower ass kissing Monty's great expectation of crossing the Rhine and ending the war all by himself, Of course it was the British first Airborne Division that fought and died against overwhelming odds, it became my profound duty to inform every one that Market Garden sounded like a salad patch for old folks, I somehow never got the connection of Market Garden having an aggressive hostile attitude, which I tagged Monty's Garden of weeds, that under the circumstances I considered was a suitable nexus to failure and overloading ones egotistical ass.

My fear was being caught and grounded, the significance of circumstances that placates to ones on survival, if I was caught listening at 2,3,4 or even 5an my world of freedom and my cigar box crystal set would be grounded right on the spot. My alarm system, was a doorknob that squeaked, a stroke of brilliance on my behalf, it was my cue to perform, I would exhale from a sleep induced state half awake, in a startled murmur I would inquire, "what's wrong," just by the thought of intrusion on my sleep, my mother's caring voice would reply, "go back to sleep darling."

Patton expressed his view!

Patton's difficulty filter, he understood the Russians, Patton quoted, "the Russian is not a European, but an Asiatic SOB, and therefore he's a devious bastard". Then without verse informed the Universe of his expressed opinion. "I have no particular desire to understand them, except to ascertain how much lead or iron it takes to kill them." Then without an afterthought concluded, "The Russian have no regard for human life and is an all out son of bitch, barbarian, and chronic drunk."

Edward R. Murrow informed the world that Patton wanted to start world war three with the Russians. I wonder how he came to that conclusion.

"Hell why not!" That was my opinion, George S. Patton old Blood and guts was my war years inspiration, I loved his famous speech. "No bastard ever won a war by dying for his country. He won it, by making the other poor dumb bastard die for his country."

To sum up Patton, in the height of battle he responded to a Chaplin, "The Magnificence, of war. When you compare war with all other forms of human endeavor for every thing else shrinks to insignificance. God help me, I do love it so!" He passed into the ages of time, to rise again when God commands it.

General Dwight Eisenhower sent an urgent message to Patton to bypass the German city of Trier because it would take four divisions to capture it. Patton's reply,

"Have taken Trier with two divisions. What do you want me to do? Give it back?"

1943 Ration books, one, two, three:

For the first time in History the United States issued Ration books, Shoe Rationing, Sugar, Coffee, canned Fruits, Vegetables, Cheese, Butter, Soups, Gas, Meat, Cooking Oils, Nylons and the list goes on and on, each individual regardless of age received a ration book, worth 48 points per ration period, and no body understood the point system, but it worked. The big slogans in 1943, "If you need it, try the black market." And the very popular poster of espionage, it displayed a spy deviously cloaked in a grimy trench coat, a hat's brim was drawn downward concealing the facial features except for the apex of the unshaven lower jaw, exposing a burning cigarette, as he lurked behind the furrowed murkiness of a tree eavesdropping into the depth of emptiness, that rendered a message of pay attention, "Lose lips, sink-ships." Copper was sought-after; the penny became a metalized travesty, the war turned the cent into a funky tin penny. "Rosie the Riveter," was on the hit parade including "That old black magic-Glen Miller," "You'll never know-Frank Sinatra," "Boogie Woogie -Tommy Dorsey," "Paper doll -Mills Brothers" and "Stormy weather – Lena Horn."

1943 the war effort was in full force:

1943 average annual salary 2,500 that's yearly, minimum wage a whooping 30 cents an hour, gasoline heading upward 19 cents a gallon with ration stamps, milk 62 cents a gallon, go figure. Television production was banned for the duration of the war; most Americans had no concept that Television existed, unless you where at the World Fair. Lights had their hours of Curfew, at sunset lined drapes of pitch black where drawn tightly closed incarcerating the radiance of light, the upper portion of car headlights where painted black, street lights went silently jet black at the sound of the nightly siren.

1944 The Home Front and Patriotism:

Mot and the tenth-street scavengers immersed in body and soul to a single-minded attitude, simply put, the war effort. I designated myself the inspired leader of the unholy five, what ever it takes scavengers of the red, white and blue, every Saturday I would round up my crew, Gloria Martin she was a hundred and thirty five pounds of supreme muscle, and had a unique ability to growl with a low guttural sound of pure unadulterated Tasmanian wolf hostility, she was indispensible, Roy Buster Jester the third, was the youngest and could cry or curse on cue, he was paramount in our dastardly undertaking. Sam Vivian Vincent a true pain in the ass, was classified a priority of necessity, for he was the proud owner of Bulla a living working mule, that pulled a full size working wagon and had access to his fathers abandoned warehouse. Chuck the refrigerator Banger was a black thirteen six foot three that crossed the scale at 337 pounds, his ability to Communicate was limited to saying nothing, or verbally threatening, "boy I'll beat your sorry little red neck ass into purple chicken mud," he was nonnegotiable about his patriotism, Yours truly Thomas Ivan Mot, was without a doubt the quintessential planner for operation scrap drive, if it was not attached or being observed we owned it! We where all sworn in blood to secrecy.

Our proficiency was unlimited in scope, alloy, aluminum, brass, copper, radiators, wire, chains, tools, car and bike parts, lawnmowers and especially rod iron stoves, We where experts at removing buried treasure from white trash back yards, old washing machines, rusted out engine blocks in less than five minuets without being detected, Roy Buster Jester was our decoy, he would stand across the street and do what ever it took, crying, cursing and on rare occasions he would remove his clothes, and moon the passing cars, that usually worked ninety nine percent of the time, on those rare occasions when he was ignored he would go stark raving insane, jumping up and down, yelling in the purest form of vulgarity that he was kidnapped, by those very individual we where ripping off. Gloria would scare the be Jesus, out of anyone heading towards our site of operation, they would stop before they turned the corner, as if death was venturing in their direction, it usually took about three to four seconds, before they hightailed in the opposite direction, her growling ability was on par with distemper and the Tasmanian wolf forging into a death stampede. Chuck the refrigerator Banger removed signs with the steel posts attached with the ease of a single huff, for he considered that as an additional bonus in the value of scrap metal, Signs had a tendency to vanish from the surrounding panorama, the no trespassing signs, keep of the grass, beware of Dog, Do Not Honk Horns, and Chuck's favorite sign, For colored only. Sam Vivian Vincent and Bulla the mule was an obvious distraction heading back and forth from the Junk Yard, to compensate for unwanted inquiries it was covered with a tarp skunk sprayed that read "road kill." Our mission was the crux of supplying the war effort and we took our responsibility seriously. We where paid in War Bond Stamps $18.75 that equaled a twenty-five dollar War Bond.

April 12,1945 the loss:

A sense of disbelief, it was being in the twilight zone, stunned adrift from reality. A hush without reprieve, as Grace Tully's words reverberated throughout the mosaic of an emotional passing that day of days, silence staggered, a slight intake of breathe sentiment sobbed the words, "our President just died." Franklyn D. Roosevelt a little after one complained of a sharp pain

and with in minuets without uttering a single word died of a
massive cerebral hemorrhage.

Harry S. Truman April 12,1945 becomes the Chief:

FDR died April 12,1945 less than a month before the
end of the European conflict, they said Harry S. Truman was the
new President, I wondered how the hell did old Harry get the Job,
I thought Henry Wallace was still Vice President.

Harry S Truman a U.S. senator in 1941 headed the
Senate Special Committee to Investigate the National Defense
Industry. The aerospace firm Curtiss-Wright was delivering
defective motors to the Army Air Corps. It discovered Curtiss-
Wright had knowingly sold leaky motors and covered it up with
forged inspection reports. The heads rolled at Curtiss-Wright, and
one general was imprisoned, Truman did not conceive without
intent as a pass. In all Harry S Truman saved American taxpayers
$15 billion today that would equate 450 Billion dollars. Most
important he prevented greed from killing thousands of our young
fighting men. Yet in the twenty first century greed supersedes the
lives of young fighting men, they where put into harms way without
protective vest and armor. It's criminal when pork-barrel politics
have shortchanged troops on the ground. Personally we should
start from ground zero, bring home our troops and let the United
Nations vote on the protection and outcome, we no longer can
afford the 2.6 Trillion that we are borrowing from China or the lives
of our American warriors. We have Plutocrats that find war
profitable, hell they sure as hell can afford to purchase a second

country, if this one goes belly up.

President Harry S. Truman great quotes:

A politician is a man who understands government. A statesman is a politician who's been dead for 15 years. Whenever a fellow tells me he's bipartisan, I know he's going to vote against me.

"The buck stops here!" Was inscribed on his desk sign, the reverse side facing Truman stated I'm from Missouri. He would turn that that sign around without a thought of hesitation when confronted with a statement of questionable fact, with a presidential verbal tweak of dictate said, "I'm from Missouri, show me!"

Truman said, "Effect of intent," he paused with an all-knowing sneer and a tilt of his head for effect inhaled to a verbal conclusion, "distorts the betrayer as protective of the Plutocrats interest and not the first amendment."

President Harry S. Truman determined to end the war in Japan without the loss of an additional million young American Soldiers. Japan believed in death before dishonor and that was not an idle threat. They where incorporating a united merger of self- holocaust before dishonor, they will fight to the last individual.

August 6, 1945 Hiroshima, the devastation of a single Atomic bomb shocked the world, General Douglas MacArthur, stated, he did not expect the Japanese would surrender under any circumstance.

On August 9 the second Atomic bomb was dropped, on

Nagasaki, President Harry S Truman publically announced, "what ever it takes I will not alter the course, and those Jap's can be assured I'll drop one every day if that's what it takes." The Japanese surrender on August 15,1945. Even Japan understood the President was from Missouri.

Old Harry was a pistol and a half; I took to him right off the bat. Just for the record, Patten has and will retain his position of my number one ass kicker but Truman is real close. The war ended in Europe and Patten died from complications in a stupid accident. Every body celebrated the wars end, the newsreel showed Time Square and this Sailor was having himself a great time with what I believe was a Nurse. August 15, 1945 Japan surrenders and the baby-boomer generation was about to go into full swing.

Truman moment of acceleration:

In May 1945, President Harry S. Truman put to pen a memorandum to the Supreme Court and the federal judiciary, a directive expressing his views. "The courts, should neither dabble in policy nor read law school theories into the law and policy laid down by the Congress."? Shakespeare said it best," For who would bear the whips and scorns of time, The oppressor's wrong, the proud man's contumely, The pangs of despised love, the law's delay the insolence of office, the patient merit spurns the unworthy takes, President Truman expressed it best.

The Secret of Tommy the Cork and Lobbyist:

Tommy Corcoran, a modern day wheeler-dealer was FDR's chief political operative known in Washington, as one of the Gold Dust Twins. His partner in crime was Benjamin V. Cohen, talent scout and new modern day Lobbyist.

Harry S. Truman in 1945 requested FBI Director J. Edgar Hoover to tap Corcoran's home and office phones. The tapes provided the distinction of the prototype modern lobbyist and influence peddler. From backroom dealings to bribery and palm greasing with major government officials, party leaders, and the Plutocratic Secret Society to banking and Wall Street. The tapes provide the art of corruption with hidden intrigue behind every door. Corcoran was without limits as he tried to bribe a Catholic Bishop, a future Supreme Court Justice, into the fray of Legislative officials, Party leaders, and the Wall Street Plutocratic fraternity.

Truman in 1949 said, "Effect of intent," he paused with an all-knowing sneer and a tilt of his head for effect, inhaled to a verbal conclusion, "distorts the betrayer as protective of the Plutocrats interest and not the first amendment."

During the last hundred years Congress and the Legislators with full verbal intent, expressed the necessity to keep a vigil over the banking practices. That's like preaching reform to the condemned. Believing a reformed crack head after three days will enforce restrictions and establish ethics, and eliminate drug distribution at his house.

Not a single Lobbyist or Politian ever died over ethics or the slap on the wrist known as being censured; that's like a hangover, take two breaths and a shot of bourbon.

In the twenty first century plus ten there are in access of twelve thousand lobbyist, the majority will come from both houses, spending over three billion dollars. That's a conservative calculated figure from a mathematical pencil. Now if you think about it, that's what you call Plutocratic control to and from a revolving White House door.

Dewey Proclaims Victory:

Harry S. Truman performed the upset of the century. Truman defeated Thomas Dewey and even the Democratic Party said, "You got to be kidding." The Chicago Tribune on November 3, 1948 headlines read Dewey defeats Truman. Ten years earlier in November 1, 1938 a rags-to the impossible dream, a horse by the name of Sea Biscuit challenged the Triple Crown Winner War Admiral, the great son of Man O' War, and the world listened on the radio to a shocking upset by a determined half pint Sea Biscuit. Harry S. Truman woke at midnight to the voice of H.V Kaltenborn reporting a different tune, "Mr. Truman is still ahead but these are returns from a few cities. When the returns come in from the country the result will show Dewey winning overwhelmingly." That day in November of 1948 Harry S. Truman became my Sea Biscuit and President for another four years.

I always considered that Harry S. Truman and Andrew Jackson had a common denominator, their ability to tell it like it was. He had the distinction in combat to keep a cool head, and never lost a single Soldier under his command in combat.

Andrew Jackson openly expressed his contempt about the Bank's arrogance to Vice President Van Buren and the press. Jackson's message to Congress was vigorously projected. He proclaimed that monopoly and special concessions for the Banks, "our rich constituents have not been content with equal protection and equal benefits, but have besought us to make them richer by act of Congress. The Bank, is trying to kill me, but I will kill it first!" He did! Hell, name me a single Politian who would dare!

Henry Clay expressed his rebuttal; "I cannot believe that Jackson is killing 2,000 Englishmen at New Orleans and that's all it took to qualify him for the difficult and complicated duties of the Presidency." Henry Clay was the luckiest man in Washington DC, Jackson never challenge Henry to a duel. Jackson had a few verbal comments pertaining to Henry Clay.

Andrew Jackson said, "After eight years as President I have only two regrets: that I have not shot Henry Clay or hanged John C. Calhoun." John C. Calhoun was Andrew Jackson's first Vice President and resigned in 1832. He would have never survived till 1833.

Jackson fought 13 duels:

Charles Dickinson had the misfortune of being the only man Old Hickory ever killed in a duel. It was supposedly over a debt of honor, then you add insult to injury, he cast aspersions on

Jackson's wife. Dickinson shot first; the bullet struck Jackson in the ribs. Jackson with a steady hand fired the fatal shot killing Dickinson, the date May 30, 1806. It was quoted on various occasions that Jackson had been wounded so frequently in duels he "rattled like a bag of marbles while dancing."

A friend from Salisbury, N.C., recalling Jackson's youth was quoted, "Jackson was the most roaring, rollicking, game-cocking, card-playing mischievous fellow, and the head of the rowdies hereabouts." No wonder he started the Democratic Party with a mule."

The art of being Presidential:

Truman when asked his opinion about Nixon without a splinter of hesitation responded, "Richard Nixon is a no good, lying bastard. He can lie out of both sides of his mouth at the same time, and if he ever caught himself telling the truth, he'd lie just to keep his mind from shorting out."

In 1948 when Truman was asked about his view on Government regulations, Harry shifted his head with that all knowing smirk, said, "Those Politian's who want the Government to regulate matters of the States, are like men who are so damn afraid of being murdered, that they simply commit suicide to avoid assassination."

You must pay the price, to secure the blessing:

Andrew Jackson stated, and if you give credence to

past historical facts, what is factual that the Senate and House of Representatives have always been seeded with party needs first, therefore pay back, and the term bipartisan is truly an art of cynical disillusion in 2012.

The Republican National Convention of 1952:

The Republican National Convention in July of 1952, my first impression was the insane atmosphere, illuminating mind boggling turmoil, as if confusion was orchestrating the delegates rank and file activities of total mayhem, yet certitude reaped a never ending flurry of intense communication, the shifting winds echoed bedlam, a sense of loyalty mutated the course of events, the roll call found defeat was self evident, Georgia, Texas, and Louisiana declared 68 additional delegates for Eisenhower the intensity increased as nine delegates hung in the balance for Taft, Minnesota's political boss Walter Judd, bellowed with determination, "Mr. Chairman, the great state of Minnesota votes goes to Eisenhower." The frenzy of voices rang the depth of desperation for presidential patronage, "Mr. Chairman!" Frantic shifted loyalty, Nixon had secured his political fortunes, the day before aboard the train was Richard Millhouse Judas converting California delegates to endorse Eisenhower. The following day Richard Millhouse Nixon was affirmed vice president.

Senator Chase was approached by a couple, with heads up, I was bedazzled, bewitched and captivated not the fact I was just introduced to Henry Luce of Time magazine, but his wife Clair Booth Luce the playwright, editor and journalist, I read her exploits over a four-month period, while reporting directly from the battlefronts. She described tragedy, from an insightful view, "a world where men have decided to die together because they are unable to find a way to live together" I was smitten, a day that altered my direction not my destiny. I was transfixed on Clair Booth when Senator Everett Dirksen of Illinois rigorously launched his finger with full vigor at Dewey from the convention floor, bellowing tunelessly, "Dewey you are personally leading the Republicans down the path to defeat," Clair Booth Luce shifted her eyes directly at me smilingly imparted words to evaluate, "Mr. Dirksen is a superior politician you know, he seams to have this ability to project himself red, white and blue on various areas of his face, except the poor fool has no earthly concept, that before this day ends, his friend and candidate Taft will be wearing, "I like Ike button." Her words rang true that night.

        The only assessment that crossed my mind was her infamous intellect, stark naked of any rational thought Clair Booth simply glided into my cerebral space, "Mot! No good deed goes punished that's if you're a Politian." I was attempting to contrive without a splinter of gray matter, when Clair Booth nudged my shoulder, with a smirk of revelation, enlightened yours truly, "Senator Mati Chase regards you as resolute, she says you have an intuitive capacity to dissect effectively what a politician thinks, from his lying intentions, which I personally insist indicates, that you must consider working for Henry [Time Magazine Luce]. I blinked without a reflective response, I said, "sure, I would like it." For the next two days I regurgitated my one liner of senility, "sure, I would like it." I swear the only insane image that appeared, I was six years old in my short pants and knee socks being offered an ice cream cone, to which I responded, "Sure, I would like it".

Senator Mati Chase's single comment was a reprieve from the dungeon of my self induced stupidity, "Henry requested, that if I didn't mind, he had a position for your talent with the Time magazine." This time I was prepared intellectually I responded, "You're firing me!"

Mati said nothing, but that look, said it all. I guess afterwards I was well indoctrinated that even partisan politics had a diversion called power, therefore anything a politician did with his pants on or off was not always determined by his fanaticism towards the subject. I didn't take the job.

Dwight David Eisenhower was nominated on the first ballot; Taft was mumbling without verbally uttering a profane or unscrupulous word, as if an aneurism of implausible was surgically removing his sanity, with out a conscious revelation of bushwhacked, Taft's political Presidential career was waylaid into the brooding eyes of injustice, annihilation was transfixed on Nixon, for he was the assassinator, Taft's undertone murmured, that sun of a bitch, down right stole my delegates, with a grimace of suicidal discontentment Taft managed to issue a partisan hand shake and congratulated Eisenhower. Two weeks latter Ike arrived without fanfare at Taft's hotel suite to continue negotiating concessions to appease and unite the GOP, it required Senator Mati two weeks to finalize Taft's discontentment to publicly congratulate Eisenhower and announce his full support; I was the silent gopher when Eisenhower arrived at the Suite; Senator Everett Dirksen from Illinois was still demanding concessions for Taft's undying support, he insisted Eisenhower pledge to balance the federal budget at all cost, and certain staffer's would receive a variety of patronage positions. Then it became apparent my departure was essential for Taft to finalize certain concessions with Eisenhower, Senator Mati Chase, had accomplish her mission.

Obligation bringing the key players to the table, Taft fulfilled his obligation as a relentless campaigner for the GOP, but perpetuated an irritation of the first order towards Richard Millhouse Nixon. Taft insinuated Nixon was "the Conductor of the Great Train Robbery," claiming Judas sold him out for the vice-presidential nomination. It was widely acknowledged Henry Cabot Lodge, Jr., informed Nixon weeks before hand that he was Eisenhower only choice for Vice President. Taft should have read John Adams summation on Aaron Burr 73 electoral votes and Thomas Jefferson 73 electoral votes, eliminated John Adams from his second term. Aaron Burr fought a duel killing Alexander Hamilton eliminating Burr from a second term as Vice President, the killing was under scrutiny, Hamilton fired first round into the air, Burr considered since it was not into the ground standard protocol of bravery and Burr shot and killed Hamilton. In 1807 Burr was tried for Treason and acquitted.

Eisenhower's darkest day:

Senator McCarthy verbally attacked General George Marshall, he was quoted; "the General is part of a conspiracy so immense, an infamy so black, as to dwarf any in the history of man."

Truman was verbally outraged, called McCarthy a

dumb son of a bitch!"

Katherine Tupper Brown, say what!

General Marshall was Chief of Staff of the United States Army from 1939 to 1946, was considered along with George Washington as one of the two most outstanding Soldiers that the county ever had. Eisenhower feared losing Wisconsin kept silent and was photographed shaking hands with McCarthy. General George Marshall forgave Eisenhower but his wife Katherine Tupper Brown Marshal did not. She was outspoken to a fault of perfection, "I told George, thank god, it wasn't your hand, or I would have had to amputate it."

Highway to heaven, the Interstate:

Eisenhower nominated for second term, The Federal-Aid Highway Act of 1956, popularly known as the Eisenhower National Interstate and Defense Highways Act, Interstate highways popped up like Rocket "80" heading West like flowing ribbon, Race With The Devil heading North on 75 for Mississippi. The car boom was the songs of the decade, "No Money Down", "Pink Thunderbird", "Road Runner", "V-8 Ford Blues", "Motor head Baby" and the ever popular "My Blue Suede Shoes, known as Elvis' Cadillac's he purchased seven that year. War and Peace, rolls mightily across the screen, in gigantic twenty foot letters declaring the greatest epics of all time! Audrey Hepburn, a single comment, to die for, Henry Fonda received second billing. Dwight D. Eisenhower the Father of the Interstate System was quoted, "I made a personal and absolute decision to see that the nation would benefit." The year 1956 and America believed and America prospered with the Interstate.

The world in 1956, harmony was affordable:

The hospital cost in 1956 for a full five-day vaginal birth experience was a whooping $207.23 that included the drugs, delivery room, baby care and the copay was 22.00 dollars out of your pocket and believe it or not you actually talked to your personal physician. In 2009 my Granddaughter's three-day stay for a vaginal birth extraordinary, the reason I emphasized extraordinary the bill was an outstanding $22,368.77 cents, that included TV and phone, copay twenty percent, you do the math. I didn't ask but I figured the accountant not the Physician congratulated her with a smile and a thank you on the way out.

Income tax for the wealthy one percent, in 1956 was a Whooping 91 percent when their income surpassed the million-dollar pinnacle of excess, in 2010 Warren Buffet paid 17.7 percent tax and his Secretary paid thirty percent. General Electric paid zero tax on 14.2 Billion and Obama claims taxing the rich will create a recession, get real we have a recession, the Government needs a class on budget spending, or learn how to tax the rich, that will afford a balance playing field.

Times are changing:

A bugle call resonated at the gravesite of General John Pershing signified the Historical 90th anniversary of the end of World War One, a solitary grave without marker was reserved at Arlington National Cemetery for the last remaining survivor, he was108 year old Veteran Frank Buckles standing upright, with a steady hand he acknowledged his generation of fallen comrades, that relinquished their youthful lives, for they paid the ultimate sacrifice on foreign soil, a silent pledge of brotherhood of those youthful faces that passed the ages of time, they have became expendable in the twenty first Century.

Once upon a time, Unconditional Heroic nobility:

The first undertaking of survival came to fruition on a battlefield O say, does that star-spangled banner yet waveO'er the land of the free and the home of the brave, where American youth spilled their blood and gave the ultimate sacrifice, their names must be etched into the fabric of the Constitution archives as Heroic nobility, they are embodied into a single spirit of sovereignty, that we so proudly hail'd. I shake the hand of every American Veteran who served; it's my soul being touched by a living historical moment of Heroic nobility, for they walked the walk.

Mary Edwards, a Civil War surgeon of the 52nd Ohio Infantry. During her assignment she served as a spy, as she crossed Confederate lines to treat civilians and pass information. She was taken prisoner in 1864 by Confederate troops and imprisoned as a spy. She received the Congressional Medal of

Honor for Meritorious Service. We have an obligation, for Mary Edwards is woven into the fabric of Patriotism; we must honor unconditional resolve of hose self-sacrificing individuals.

The first African American recipient of the Medal of Honor in the Civil War was William Harvey Carney, despite being shot in the face, shoulders, arms, and legs, refused to let the American flag touch the ground, we inherited a nation of Heroic Individuals and the Supreme Court interprets to defame a Fallen hero, as freedom of speech, he was an American Marine that paid the ultimate price, first and foremost without their sacrifice, we would have no Constitution or Supreme Court.

William R. Caddy Marine Private first class sacrificed his life to save the lives of his platoon leader and platoon sergeant. How in God's name can we degrade the fabric of fallen Patriots?

Jack Harrell Lucas Marine Private first class covered two Japanese grenades with his body. Survived the blast of the one that exploded. Youngest recipient since the Civil War; turned 17 just 5 days before Iwo Jima D-Day.   Douglas E. Dickey Marine Private first class sacrificed his life to save several fellow Marines by diving on a grenade and absorbing the explosion with his body.

Pfc. Adriana Alvarez, 20, of San Benito, Texas, she died Feb. 10 in Baghdad, of injuries sustained while supporting combat operations.

Army Major Alan Greg Rogers Intelligence Officer, 40 died January 27, 2008 in Bagdad of wounds received in combat, a civil rights activist in the gay military community, the first gay combat fatality of Operation Iraqi Freedom.

Lance Cpl. Matthew A. Snyder, 20 of Finksburg, Maryland, died in a vehicle accident in Al Anbar province, Iraq. Was targeted by the Westboro Baptist Church, which claims military deaths are punishment for America's tolerance of homosexuality.

Whereas disregard and contempt for human rights have resulted in barbarous acts, which have outraged the conscience of mankind, thereby the highest aspiration is to honor our fallen Hero's, above all other sanctions, regardless of gender, color, ethnic, sexual preference or religion they are the Nobility of America.

Westboro Baptist Church, freedom of contempt

Its unconscionable eight Supreme Court Justices categorized contempt as freedom of derision. A draped American Flag signifies the Holy Unity of a fallen Hero's ultimate sacrifice. The inherent symbolism of patriotism validates the foundation of our Constitutional survival, personification with failure of respect for a Hero's ultimate offering; It's time to mark the inalienable sacrifice of that illustrious fraternity, a death count without title or respect, outranks human dignity, their final attainment abandonment without honor or respect. Suicide became their final death count. Freedom is never more than one generation away from extinction. It must be fought for, protected, or one day we will spend our sunset years telling our children and our children's children what it was once like in the United States when "we the people" were Patriots.

The end of Camelot:

November 22, 1963 Kennedy assassinated, LBJ becomes the thirty-sixth President, and the world morns the end of an American Camelot, a period of grandeur, with adversity and then the web of the mirror crack'd, Tennyson's, "The lady of Shalott," She look'd down to Camelot. Out flew the web and floated wide; the mirror crack'd from side to side; "The curse is come upon me," cried The Lady of Shalott; A laud rendering to a beloved First Lady, Jackie O.

Eagle Chief (Letakos-Lesa) Pawnee:

All things in the world are two. In our minds we are two, good and evil. With our eyes we see two things, things that are fair and things that are ugly.... We have the right hand that strikes and makes for evil, and we have the left hand full of kindness, near the heart. One foot may lead us to an evil way; the other foot may lead us to a good. So are all things two. Political corruption was born into the fiber of the American heritage, the embodiment of American heritage is sacrifice so all things of two must be weighed for their value

I'll be back in 2013, A Universe beyond!

"So be it!"

www.ingramcontent.com/pod-product-compliance
Lightning Source LLC
Chambersburg PA
CBHW050114280326
41933CB00010B/1095